Body Trauma TV

Body Trauma TV
The New Hospital Dramas

Jason Jacobs

 Publishing

For H and H

First published in 2003 by the
British Film Institute
21 Stephen Street, London W1T 1LN

The British Film Institute promotes greater understanding of,
and access to, film and moving image culture in the UK.

Cover Design: Wheelhouse Creative
Set by Wyvern 21 Ltd, Bristol
Printed in the UK by St Edmundsbury Press, Bury St Edmunds, Suffolk

British Library Cataloguing-in-Publication Data

A catalogue record for this book is available from the British Library
ISBN 0–85170–881–1 (pbk)
ISBN 0–85170–880–3 (hbk)

Contents

Acknowledgments

Sincere thanks first of all to my editor Andrew Lockett for his patience and generosity.

I began watching TV hospital dramas regularly at the same time as I started lecturing full time in the Department of Film and Television Studies at the University of Warwick in 1994. A year later I was teaching those shows as part of the television component of a course called 'Film Aesthetics', and continued to do so until I resigned from Warwick in 2000. During that time many of the students on that course contributed and enriched my thinking about just what might be new and different in the new hospital dramas; they also made teaching a pleasure to do. I want to thank all of those students for that, especially: Rachel Moseley, Tom Richmond, Ian Goode, Paul Long, Kerrie Lofthouse, Nick Potamitis, Caroline Smith, James Pratt, Jon Ashton, J. Blakeson, Stuart Henderson, Mark Jones, Luella Forbes and Lesley-Ann Barcroft. I would also like to thank my former colleagues in the Department of Film and Television Studies for their company and inspiration, in particular José Arroyo, Charlotte Brunsdon, Victor Perkins, Richard Dyer, Ginette Vincendeau, Ed Gallafent, Ros Jennings, Neill Potts, Peter McCluskie, Elaine Lenton, Jim Penn and Frank Gibson. Helen Wheatley and Catherine Johnson helped to make thinking and talking about television much more than I imagined it could be. I'm particularly grateful to my friend Charlotte for the video 'dowry' and for treating this with such encouragement.

I continued researching and writing and finally completed the book while working in the School of Film, Media and Cultural Studies at Griffith University. My students and colleagues there also contributed to my thinking about television, in particular Jane Roscoe, Amanda Howell and Tom O'Regan; Peter Thomas and Jason Wilson listened to me when they didn't have to. Thanks also to Brett Wiltshire.

I would also like to acknowledge the brilliance of the 'alt.tv.er' team (<www. digiserve.com/er/erdex.html>) for the reviews and information they maintain, without which things would have been much more difficult for me. In particular the comments and opinions of Phyl Behrer, Mike Sugimoto, Scott Hollifield and Dave Ragsdale helped to confirm and inspire my own critical directions. It is without doubt the best website devoted to a television show.

An early version of Chapter 2 was presented to the Midlands Television Research Group, and I'm grateful to them for receiving it with interest. Parts of Chapter 2 were originally published in 'Issues of Judgement and Value in Television Studies', *International Journal of Cultural Studies*, vol.4, no.4 (Sage: December 2001). Parts of the Introduction have been published in the 'Hospital Dramas' chapter of Glen Creeber (ed.), *The Television Genre Book* (London: BFI, 2001).

Valerie Spall supported me throughout the difficult time of writing and I am grateful for her loyalty and love and hard work. Henry and Hannah, as always, were good to come home to and hard to leave – this is for you.

Introduction

The human body is the best picture of the human soul.[1]

This book is about television hospital fiction that uses body trauma and medical treatment as the source of its drama. In their combination of a fast-paced explicit depiction of injury and illness and detailed attention to the working and personal lives of medical professionals, shows such as *ER* (NBC, 1994–), *Chicago Hope* (CBS, 1994–2000) and *Cardiac Arrest* (BBC, 1994–6) that achieved prominence and popularity during the mid-1990s constituted a distinctive development in the medical drama genre. Although the hospital setting was nominally a place of healing, in these shows it resembled a war zone. In scenes of emergency and medical 'action' the styles and spectacles of 1990s Hollywood action cinema were transplanted to interior spaces where awkward confinement was juxtaposed with the speedy mobility of the camera and an environment densely populated by sick, bleeding and dying patients. This setting was a ripe source of accident and injury dramatised as part of the everyday routines and pressures of working life. For the audience, these dramas connected with and nurtured a popular fascination with decay, death and the destruction of the body. They presented a 'morbid gaze' – the visualisation of the horrible but routine body trauma – within a context of procedural and ethical rules, and the professional language of science and medicine.

For example, towards the end of the live episode of *ER*, 'Ambush', Dr Mark Greene (Anthony Edwards) is called to an emergency cardiac resuscitation where we discover a junior doctor, John Carter (Noah Wyle), desperately trying to revive an elderly patient.[2] Earlier in the episode we saw Carter developing a good-humoured relationship with this character (a nursing home Lothario); suddenly and unexpectedly his heart has stopped and Carter is trying to bring him back to life using electric shocks on his chest:

Greene: [running in] What happened?

Carter: [*administering defibrillation*] He went into in fib! Clear! ... I shocked him
    five times, he went asystole ... gave him a high dose epi and atropine ... [*to
    nurse*] Charge it again! Clear!

Greene: Why didn't you call me?

Carter: I did.

Greene: That was two minutes ago.

Carter: I was following his ACO algorithm – I thought I could handle it. Charge it
    again! Clear!

Greene: Call it Dr Carter!

Carter: Charge it again!

[*Greene turns off the machine*]

Carter: [*quietly*] Time of death 9.56.

Greene: [*angry*] Call an attending when there's a full arrest: you get help, you don't
    try and play the hero!

Carter: [*sad*] I've done it before ...

Greene: That was up in surgery, you work here now.

[*Camera favours Carter, who is moving away, upset. Greene is checking Carter's notes*]

Carter: Did I miss anything?

Greene: Not that I can see.

Carter: [*very upset*] I'm sorry I didn't think I was gonna lose him. [*Turns and walks
    away along a busy corridor*]

Both doctors walk away, the nurses begin stripping the body of its IV leads and
monitor pads while the camera moves in to a close-up of the dead man's face;
amid the background noise of the hospital on the soundtrack we hear a very
young baby, perhaps a newborn, crying.

The sequence exemplifies some of the key characteristics of body trauma
television: it is fast; it signals trauma as a sudden contingency of the body which
is the source of drama (the patient simply 'went asystole'); it situates this trauma
in relation to the reactions, behaviour and feelings of the medical staff rather
than the patient or his family; it evolves from an 'action scene' depicting
emergency treatment, to a primarily dialogue-based scene, allowing the doctors
to reflect on the causes and consequences of that action. This is depicted with
attention to the accurate medical and corporeal details so that as electric shocks
are administered they make the patient's body jump and his head jerk, a
dramatic image of the body between life and death, between artificially
stimulated movement and grim reluctant stillness. The camera acts as both
observer and embodied witness to the events shown, reacting to the events by
variously reframing on the patient, Carter and Greene.

Is Carter a 'bad doctor' because his patient dies? It is an ethical possibility

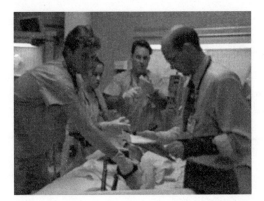

'Clear!': John Carter performs
defibrillation on a dying patient in *ER*,
'Ambush'

implied by his 'Did I miss anything?' but mitigated by his compassionate attachment to his patient, 'I didn't think I was gonna lose him'. The distribution of our sympathies is made uncomfortable: because of the extreme nature of the event itself – a man dying – it is difficult to feel at ease aligning ourselves either with Greene's angry admonition or Carter's initial sincere-but-wrong self-confidence that led him to ignore hospital procedure and go it alone. The death of a patient is the pretext for a discussion about procedure so that ethical issues are framed within the specific context of working practices. Viewer proximity is distributed between our sympathy for the dead patient and Carter's inexperienced emotional response to it.

The motifs, patterns and characteristics in this example from *ER* can be found in many other medical dramas: there is the pace that is responsive to contingency, action that evolves into reflection, and the focus on the doctor's reactions. Repeated shocks, the monotone whine of the EKG monitor and the reluctance to let a life go are also familiar elements of the hospital drama narrative and *mise en scène*. Yet familiarity with the genre offers the opportunity for the programme to create subtle effects and variations that go against our expectations or to 'tweak' familiar moments for novel effects. In this example the pathos of the sounds of a baby crying juxtaposed with the dead face of the old man emphasises the idea of 'cycle of life', death and birth and the journey from one to the other. The potential sentimentality and clichéd nature of such a juxtaposition is troubled, however, by its context. Just before the close-up of the man's face we see an annoyed nurse griping that he needs the death certificate signed – this sets up a contrast in scale between *his* urgent need to fulfil the requirements of administrative formality and those of the dying patient's body a few moments before. A man's sudden death is also the cause of a trivial irritation. The movement of the camera towards and then pausing on the dead man's face signals *its* fascination with the human body and its death. In this (live) episode the images we see are produced by a documentary crew that has been filming in the ER that night so the movement to close-up is *embodied* – moving close to the dead man is a manifestation of the cameraman's morbid voyeurism.[3] The movement of the camera to rest on the dead man's face offers not only the juxtaposition of death with the sounds of new life, but also the impulse, revealed in the viewpoint, to capture a powerful image of recent death. In doing this the scene asks the audience to reflect on *our* motives and pleasures in seeing and hearing this. Why is the spectacle of traumatised and dying bodies dramatic and compelling?

The rest of the book is a critical account of the attractions of body trauma television and the elaboration of a genre that has worked over (discovered) a significant aspect of the television medium: its tendency to exhibit, dramatise and work over trauma, fragmentation and loss. This tendency has manifested in other genres as well, but the medical drama, with its natural focus on the body as a site and source of dramatic events, has been able to explore it with special intensity. Why are *these* incidents chosen as dramatically significant rather than, for instance, those of growth and revival? An explanation for this would account for why the cameraman chooses to image a dead man rather than a newborn child; it is an explanation that underpins the interests of what follows. To begin with, I want to outline three broad historical stages in the development of the hospital drama genre: paternal, conflict and apocalyptic.

Paternal

During the 1950s the massive expansion in healthcare spending and medical research in the UK and US coincided with the consolidation of television as a major domestic leisure pursuit. The first instances of the hospital-based television medical drama were exemplified by shows such as *Medic* (US, 1954–5), *Emergency – Ward 10* (UK, 1957–67) and *Dr Kildare* (US, 1961–6). These shows were based around an anthology format with self-contained weekly episodes and regular central characters; they were respectful of the growing power and authority of the medical institutions and took care to show that, whatever the outcome in individual cases, medical progress was inexorable. As well as provide regular doses of drama, the shows sought to augment public trust in the medical profession; the American Medical Association, and the British Medical Association, who supplied advisors that checked scripts for medical accuracy, underwrote their stamp of quality and authenticity. They also had a vested interest in making sure that their profession was represented in a positive light, and it was important for these authorities that the shows did not encourage anxiety and hypochondria. According to Dr Meyrick Emrys-Roberts, medical advisor for *Emergency – Ward 10*, the important thing was, 'to make sure that the doctors were shown in the best light possible so that the public wouldn't lose their faith in medicine'.[4]

Reassurance was personified in the figure of the infallible, capable doctor and in the early shows the focus was on the individual doctor's central role in healing people; typically the doctors were white males at the centre of authority in the hospital or practice. Early hospital-based dramas aimed for realism and accuracy in their depiction of medical procedure (within the constraints of censorship and taste), balancing this against the gravitational pull of melodrama understood at the time by some in the television industry as a capitulation to the trivial appeal of soap opera.

In the 1960s the hospital doctor was depicted as working as part of a team, usually emphasising the paternal relationship between young doctor and his experienced teacher. For example, *Dr Kildare* exemplified the nurturing 'father-son' relationship between Kildare (Richard Chamberlain) and his mentor and superior, Dr Gillespie (Raymond Massey). Based on the character in Max Brand's pulp novels, Dr James Kildare was first seen on the big screen in *Interns Can't Take Money* (Paramount, 1937), a film that anticipated many of the concerns of later television hospital dramas. It was a generic hybrid (medical, melodrama, gangster) that foregrounded Kildare's ambition to combine a mastery of contemporary medical technology with compassion for his patients. During the 1940s and 50s a series of B-pictures made by MGM, featuring Kildare and Gillespie, further popularised the character and the genre. Like many of the new hospital dramas it was set in a teaching hospital and established the senior/junior doctor relationship as a nurturing one where wisdom and knowledge were passed down without conflict. The education of a young idealistic doctor was both instructional for the viewer and a way of showing how the eternal values of medical care and wisdom were reproduced in action. Kildare was not presented as an aloof member of a medical priesthood but as a modern professional who was committed, sincere and caring. The *Kildare* movies also consolidated what was to become a pattern of the television shows whereby patients (and their illness) were vehicles for the exploration of particular moral, ethical, familial and legal issues.

The television version was similarly careful to represent Kildare and Gillespie as modern professionals rather than members of a medical priesthood. In terms of narrative, *Dr Kildare* combined character development with the treatment of a variety of patients so that human relationships were seen through the lens of acute medical problems. It is also a striking example of the hospital drama's early tendency to juxtapose glamour with morbidity. The TV network's appetite for a large audience explains the casting of a handsome young actor like Chamberlain, but the proximity of attractive actors to life or death matters provided an enhancement to that glamour, particularly as Kildare himself was largely oblivious to his appeal (although those around him and the show's cameras were not). In *Kildare* the appeal of its star is juxtaposed with his treatment of the anonymous sick so that the popular face of television medicine conflated benevolent healthcare with good looks. In the early seasons Kildare himself mostly ignored romantic opportunities that regularly internalised Chamberlain's popular appeal to the audience in the narrative in favour of another suitor – Science.

Kildare's work at Blair General was about the application of the best in medical-scientific knowledge, and even the most tragic events could be co-opted to serve this noble aspiration. In 'A Life for a Life', a senior medical figure Dr Maxwell Becker (played by James Mason, in a manner that leaves no doubt as to his character's belief in himself as Medicine's answer to God) is paralysed from the waist down by a car accident and, faced with the consequent diminished potency (as well as his drunken floozy of a wife who flirts with Kildare) and kidney failure, is on the brink of committing suicide using a gun he has managed to conceal. Kildare intervenes just before Becker pulls the trigger and, leaning over the bed, he argues that Becker should stay alive for the benefit of medical science:

> You're a scientist, a realist, a facer of facts – alright, let's face some facts! You probably won't walk again; you probably will go into uraemic poisoning and I may not be able to pull you through it. In any case the poison in your kidneys will begin to poison your mind, hallucinate things, even *your* mind Dr Becker! But before that we have time – time to find things out about your paralysis. *You* – feeling, saying what you sense – writing it down – keeping the records for science. A couple of days, a week in the clear maybe before the uraemic poisoning sets in, if it does set in. When will science have a chance like that again, Dr Becker, when?[5]

This is primarily an appeal to Becker's, rather than his own, dedication to science and Kildare's speech has the immediate objective of preventing his patient from killing himself. Whereas Becker embodied the aristocratic distance of the old medical priesthood, Kildare's interest in medical science is about helping patients rather than Science alone: he is the humanised, friendly face of medical-scientific progress. In many ways Becker's 'punishment' in this episode is in collapsing the usual distance between scientific observer and patient, so that he studies the disease from the inside out. Unlike his relationship with Gillespie, whose patient teaching and soft-spoken wisdom he respects, Kildare is in immediate conflict with Becker who is interested in cases insofar as they contribute and develop the range of medical-scientific knowledge. Hence Becker, and characters like him, functioned to demonstrate the distinction between the traditional way of treating medical cases which privileged scientific progress over all else, and modern healthcare practices and attitudes exemplified by Kildare who combined scientific learning with compassion for his patients. This distinction did not necessarily reflect the real world of medical practice but in instances like this it certainly addressed a widespread perception of medical science as something that was old, distant and unconcerned with the 'person behind the body' while showing a modern alternative attitude. In this way the paternal hospital dramas promoted a reassuring vision of a world healed by a modernising medical science represented by its caring and capable emissaries in the hospital wards.

Conflict

Young people who defined themselves in conflict with the old establishment and its personifications populated the counter-culture movements of the 1960s and 70s. At the same time, television networks needed to harvest this unpredictable youth demographic and they therefore sought to integrate ideas, feelings and slogans of the counter-culture in sanitised ways into their programmes. For example, *Medical Center* (CBS, 1971) modifies the paternal teaching relationship of *Kildare* to one of 'mutual respect' between senior and junior doctor, an acknowledgment that youth 'had something to say' too. This show, like other hospital dramas of the 1970s, included frequent explicitness in the discussion of medical and social 'problems': abortion, homosexuality, rape, drug addiction, artificial insemination, venereal disease, issues that had been more or less excluded from the earlier shows on the grounds of taste and audience sensitivity. We can understand this explicitness in terms of greater cultural liberalisation but it is also part of a desire to map societal anxieties onto the body. In these shows, the body was not only a site for the application of benevolent medical science, but also a physical canvas for the display of the consequences of the transgression of traditional morality and mores. Illness and injury continued to be catalysts for the exploration of human relationships, emotions, desires and morals, and as Anne Karpf argues they retained an aspiration to reassurance not about medical science so much as the future of society itself:

> In the 1960s and 1970s the United States and Europe were undergoing enormous social upheaval, especially in family relationships ... The medical drama provided a wise man to mediate family relationships and restore harmony. And while dominant values were being contested, and chasms of difference opening up between the different generations, between black and white, between men and women, the doctor shows reasserted social hope and stability.[6]

'I am 20,000 miles from home,
working as an extra in a war movie
with this guy's blood dripping into my
boot.' Hawkeye (Alan Alda) in
M*A*S*H

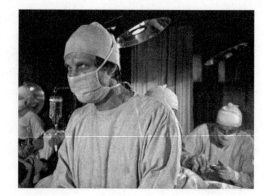

To some extent *M*A*S*H* (CBS, 1972–83) in its endorsement of liberal humanism confirms this claim. Although primarily considered a sitcom, *M*A*S*H* was also the first hospital drama that routinely rejected and ridiculed consensus-based depictions of medical care. In it we see doctors with no control over their environment, three miles from the front line of the Korean War, and healing patients so that they could go back to the front and kill or be killed. *M*A*S*H* revitalised the form by mixing black comedy with the humanist despair of Hawkeye (Alan Alda) so that the comedy had an ironic and desperate edge, exemplified in the title song, 'Suicide is Painless'. The doctors were no longer fighting against abstract forces of disease or the contingency of accidental injuries: their environment – including the wounded patients – was part of the problem and contributed to their absurd despair. *M*A*S*H* is probably the most influential show in terms of the thematic tone of the 1990s hospital dramas since, like them, it used the hospital setting as a means to explore existential issues that went beyond healthcare and into the 'sickness' at the heart of America. For example, in one episode the OR is overflowing with patients and shaking to the explosions of shellfire outside; Frank Burns, the pipsqueak straight surgeon calls out, 'I hope we're givin' it them good, those little yellow reds.' Hawkeye responds with a bitter attack on modern life in America implying as he does so that progress has its own cost to that nation's health:

> *Hawkeye:* I just don't know why they're shooting at us. All we want to do is bring them democracy and white bread. Transplant the American Dream. Freedom, achievement, hyper-acidity. Affluence, flatulence, technology, tension. The inalienable right to an early coronary sitting at your desk while plotting to stab your boss in the back. That's entertainment!
>
> *Burns:* You are certifiably insane!
>
> *Hawkeye:* Gee, I can't understand why – here I am 20,000 miles from home, working as an extra in a war movie with this guy's blood dripping into my boot.

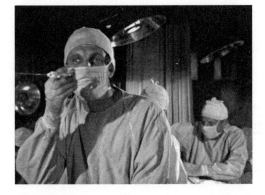

Hawkeye fools around in the OR

Hawkeye's estimation of the war as both ultimately based on faulty assumptions about the appeal of America, and as something that is staged, is an early example of the lack of faith in nation and self that medical dramas would later explore. It is also notable that he frames these witticisms in the context of a reading of Hollywood, and television as a dream factory ('That's entertainment!', 'an extra in a war movie') which implies that the show is well aware of the difficulties of deploying critical social comment in the context of a television network system that discouraged it. But Hawkeye's comments stand in the face of accusations of insanity (and network censorship) because they are part of an attack on modernity in general (technology, tension, etc.) rather than America alone. It is a tendency we see developed in the new hospital dramas of the 1990s where criticism is similarly articulated around general problems of the human condition in modern society.

The most obvious similarity between *M*A*S*H* and 1990s hospital dramas was the ensemble cast. Instead of the single-doctor star (supported by older parental figures such as Dr Gillespie) in the 1970s and 80s we begin to see ward-based ensemble dramas. It is as if the impact of particular medical crises and their moral ramifications could no longer be healed by one figure, so multiple characters oiled the wheels of multi-tiered narrative structures that were used to weave more complex dispersals of viewpoint between patients and doctors.

The focus on medical staff facing the negative impact of a hostile environment was continued in the UK with Paula Milne's gritty *Angels* (BBC, 1975–83), which followed the chaotic lives of student nurses, and G. K. Newman's *The Nation's Health* (Channel 4, 1984), the latter depicting a corrupt and failing National Health Service. These medical dramas kept closely to the twin demands of UK television at the time: that they should aspire to the accuracy (and assumed political progressiveness) of social realism, and that they downplay sentiment and overt displays of visual style in their presentation. Newman's drama came closest to *M*A*S*H* thematically in its downbeat assumption that madness was an appropriate response to an absurd situation, but it remained grounded in a grim and bitter landscape of social and economic decline reinforced by an inexpressive camera style and bland interiors.

This downbeat tone continued in two key hospital dramas of the 1980s: *St Elsewhere* (NBC, 1982–8) and *Casualty* (BBC, 1986–). *St Elsewhere* was set in an under-funded Boston teaching hospital, St Eligius, and was heavily influenced by the visual and narrative style of *Hill Street Blues* (NBC, 1981), not least in the deployment of ensemble casts as the basis for multi-narrative episodes. The medical staff were less potent than ever, neither heroic nor cool under pressure, and they were also the primary focus of narrative drama. Patients were rapidly becoming background devices for the development of central characters where we see a mainstreaming of 'existential issues' (yuppie angst) such as the spiritual burden of doing a high-pressure job: doctors were not only more fragile, but more introspective about their failing potency.

Casualty is an ensemble hospital drama that began with a campaigning tone in relation to the UK welfare cuts of the 1980s; however, from the beginning it maintained an overtly moralistic tone in relation to its patients. Both *Casualty* and *St Elsewhere* showcased their sensitivity in relation to socio-medical issues (AIDS, homosexuality, organ donation, euthanasia) and both were dress rehearsals for the speedier dramas of the mid-1990s. They also exemplify the different styles of British and US television: *St. Elsewhere* relied on a cinematic house style that emphasised chaos and complexity, underwritten by solid acting and writing. *Casualty* exemplified British cinema and television's obsession with montage as a preferred dramatic technique, using teasing vignettes of potential casualties and crosscutting between them and the casualty ward into which they would soon (perhaps) be delivered. Both shows flaunted a visceral explicitness in their depiction of injuries; *Casualty* in particular frequently used recent news stories as plot stimulants. Both depicted their medical staff as fragile, sensitive workers caught between a rigid bureaucracy, budget cutbacks, and the overwhelming burden of dealing with the medical wages of societal sin and everyday violence.

Apocalypse
Casualty is interesting because it spans the period of transition when new medical dramas began to assert themselves in the 1990s. But, although *Casualty* adopted and, in some episodes, anticipated the concerns of new medical drama it remained firmly constrained by the success of its peculiar and rigid formula and by its position as a mainstream evening family show. Nevertheless, it is important to note that 1990s hospital dramas obviously did not completely reject traditional

generic interests (how could they?), but instead intensified and modified some of the latent or underdeveloped features of earlier instances of the genre.

For example, *Cardiac Arrest* represents a shift of attention in the genre from a concern with the patient and nation as victims of welfare cuts, to a concern with junior doctors as victims of a pernicious healthcare system, and who also suffer the weight of their depoliticised 'grunge' generation.[7] The central characters are junior doctors in their early to mid-twenties who are confronted by monstrous senior doctors (who represent a corrupt, macho medical profession), sleep deprivation, debt and the tyranny of their bleepers. They are also faced with interference from new hospital managers fuelled by the ideology and management-speak of the business sector from which they were recruited. In *Cardiac Arrest* the medical/moral education exemplified in the interaction of Gillespie and Kildare is banished to the realms of naïve utopianism. *Cardiac Arrest* represents the first of the new hospital dramas because its speed and the intensity of its despair and cynicism were distinctive departures from earlier attempts that positioned the UK healthcare service within a realist frame. Indeed, *Cardiac Arrest* was not averse to visual and narrative stylisation or overt depictions of routine medical negligence.

Despite *Cardiac Arrest*'s success in the UK and Australia, the new hospital dramas only achieved widespread public visibility with the premiere seasons of two US shows in 1994. *ER* (NBC) and *Chicago Hope* (CBS) were both set in Chicago hospitals and boasted ensemble casts. *Chicago Hope* was created by TV veteran David E. Kelley, *ER* by 'auteur-imports' Steven Spielberg and Michael Crichton. *ER* won the ratings battle and was the more successful of the two throughout the late 1990s (*Chicago Hope* was axed in 1999). While *Casualty* and *Chicago Hope* continued to popularise a new medical morality of 'healthy living', 'health eating' and 'safe sex', *ER*'s nuanced and complex storytelling was able to balance its often-unbearable assertions of despair and hopelessness with the promise of potential, if short-lived, rewards of collegiality, friendship and romance.

1994 is a good year to locate the beginning of new hospital dramas since *ER* and *Chicago Hope* were premiered, against one another in what is regarded as the best weekday prime-time slot in the US (Thursday 10pm) and therefore publicly foregrounded the inauguration of the new medical drama. What was 'new' about them?

The style and address of new hospital drama had a rawness, explicitness, pace, cynicism and despair that was effectively normalised in their narratives. However, the 'traditional genre' remains in play as a point of reference as much as departure, most prominently in those shows that do not consistently use the hospital as the primary setting for their narrative events (such as *Doogie Howser,*

MD [ABC, 1989–93] and *Dr Quinn, Medicine Woman* [CBS, 1993–8]). Others, like *Casualty*, have developed their visual style and narrative in response to shows such as *ER* (a comparison of *Casualty* episodes in the late 1990s with earlier ones shows them using steadicam more often and having more densely populated background planes). *ER* is able to mix genre-traditional elements, such as the redemptive delivery of a child by a doctor who has just witnessed carnage, with genre-innovative ones. It is a question of degree, and overall, shows such as *Cardiac Arrest*, *ER* and *Chicago Hope* have used genre-traditional elements as a point of departure and a baseline for their distinctive treatment of familiar medical situations.

The structure of this book addresses the important differences of the new hospital dramas. The first chapter considers the importance of context for the genre, concentrating on the impact of wider socio-cultural changes in relation to healthcare issues and their representation on television. The 1990s represented an unprecedented intensification of the medicalisation of everyday life: regular health scares, the theori- sation of the 'risk society', the promotion of 'healthy living' (by the government and its agencies as well as by television shows) as a moral as much as a medical impera- tive all contributed to a popular engagement with the fictional depiction of medical practice. At the same time, with the collapse of the old distinctions between Left and Right, and the narrowing of politics to a more or less managerial role, any sense of social change was frequently collapsed into a concern with the body itself. As Michael Fitzpatrick argues:

> For the mass of people, the main effect of the stagnation of society has been to foster a sense of apprehension and diminished expectations for the future. If collective aspirations are no longer viable, then the scope for individual aspirations is also reduced. The contemporary preoccupation with the body is one consequence of this: if you cannot do much about society or your place in it, at least you can mould your own body according to your own inclinations. The consequences of this narcissistic outlook range from the fads for body-building, tattooing and body-piercing to the increasing prevalence of morbid conditions of self-mutilation, anorexia and bulimia … The intense social concern about health is closely related to the cult of the body: once you give up on any prospect of achieving progress in society, your horizons are reduced to securing your own physical survival.[8]

The increase in television shows that foreground the benefits of personal makeovers (clothes, skin, hair, breasts, penis, etc.) reflect this concentration on the body as a site of limited change. For the new hospital dramas of the 1990s, the sense of humanist despair and impotence in the face of illness, disease and injury hinted at in earlier shows such as *M*A*S*H* became normalised as an everyday feature of the genre. This despair and helplessness in the face of fate is captured by Susan Sontag's observations about the impact of AIDS on the western imagination which she argues exemplifies the permanent anxiety about the immanent disaster that is modern life: 'A permanent modern scenario: apocalypse looms ... and it doesn't occur. And it still looms ... Apocalypse is now a long-running serial: not "Apocalypse Now" but "Apocalypse From Now On".' [9]

The new forms of television realism that emerged in the early 1990s were indicative of a voyeuristic interest in everyday life – television's 'ambition to see everything' exemplified in 'reality TV' and workplace documentaries. Many of these shows used rapid transitions between different spaces, stories and people within an overall stylistic umbrella that stressed immediacy and authenticity. What made such shows appealing was a combination of voyeurism and reactive immediacy to contingent events – the crime, crash, emergency, argument – so that the camera seemed as if taken by surprise. Hospital dramas appropriated these stylistic trends and overhauled them to suit their own fictional themes and interests, particularly in their rapid alternation between action scenes depicting emergency medical treatment and those of reflection and introspection. The 'action mode' of hospital drama explores the radical contingency of accidents and the 'sudden turn for the worse' that can befall patients. These sequences are rendered in a fluid, restless visual style which is complemented by medical 'techno-babble' that accompanies the immediacy of injury and treatment. Chapter 2 explores this mode as a significant marker of generic difference with earlier shows. Action scenes are intertwined with moments of reflection, where doctors and nurses assess the risks and consequences of a medical procedure for the patients and for themselves. Both modes energise the spaces of the hospital casualty ward (as it is known in the UK) or emergency room (US) in ways that allow their ensemble casts and multi-tiered narrative patterns to interact with the arrival of new trauma cases.

The appropriation of visual modes and styles from reality television and action cinema may be contrasted with the serialised-series form of the shows which allows particular episodes to develop continuing stories and characters over time. The short-term immediacy of trauma inhabited a familiar world where patterns of personal development were developed in relation to the treatment of emergencies. Combining fast-paced action with an observational-realist mode that follows workplace behaviour and the long-term character development associated with soap operas is part of the appeal of the new hospital dramas since the dramatic possibilities of each allows considerable variation in tone and pace of narrative development. In the earlier example from *ER* the 'action' of a heart attack prompts a discussion of workplace procedure, and ends on Carter's melodramatic expression/suppression of emotion (according to Andy Medhurst, 'For audiences doctoring is unbridled melodrama'[10]). By patterning these modes effectively body trauma television can synthesise the complex pleasures of spectacle, realism and melodrama.

Melodramatic themes are usually associated with the personal sphere, but in body trauma television these too are anchored in tension with the demands of the workplace. Most of them are set in teaching hospitals allowing the narrative to foreground personal and professional development as part of a teaching and learning process. The immediacy of a single trauma case is integrated with the long-term training, learning and teaching of the medical staff, and for them this case may be a test of skill, development and attitude. Chapter 3 considers the importance of this process as a way of attuning the audience to the 'rules of the genre' as much as it is a device for exploring conflict between medical staff. In the *ER* scene, Carter is a junior doctor whose confidence in his skills leads him to breach correct procedure; Greene's response as his senior ('Call an attending when there's a full arrest; you get help, you don't try and play the hero') is an instance of instruction – a form of 'this is how we do things around here'. Teacher-student relations are an important means of dramatising the reproduction of knowledge and generational conflict as well as workplace procedure. Watching doctors who 'play the hero' (and fail in the role) or 'care too much' can make for exhilarating and moving drama; in the example from *ER* above, Carter's individual initiative clashes with the correct procedure, although it is also clear that Carter's shaken response is intended to redeem him in the eyes of his superior and the audience.

Articulating the personal as it intersects with the professional makes workplace romances potentially potent narrative devices, and romance has a tough time finding full expression in a world punctuated by the regular ingress of damaged patients. The possibility of romance and the enjoyment of the friendship of co-workers balances and sharpens the somewhat grim tone of many action and reflection scenes. The medical staff come into contact with many different patients from a range of backgrounds who provide the pretext for further character development; patients may often operate as dramatic 'reflectors' for the medical staff by representing or articulating dimensions of their predicament, identity or situation that is reflected back to them in an acute form. Carter's treatment of the old man and his attachment to him is credible not least because they share certain traits – they are both single with regularly fulfilled sexual appetites. Patients like this often provide the pretext for medical staff to reflect on their own situations; they are 'reflectors' of the issues that are pressing on the doctors who attend to them. Chapter 4 examines the way in which patients are used to contribute to character development.

Chapter 5 considers one of the more unpleasant features of the new hospital dramas: their fascination with narratives of death and decay. The death of a patient is one particularly potent instance where the convolution of professional and personal attachments can be articulated. Medical dramas in the past had tended to promote harmony between staff and patients and were sensitive to the possibility that graphic depictions of illness and injury might alienate, offend and disturb the television audience. For these shows the patient's 'passing away' was confined to off-screen space. Concealment rather than explicitness and reassurance rather than disturbance were often the desired effects.[11] However, as the *ER* scene demonstrates, the possibility that doctors could actually kill their patients through negligence, omission, or incorrect procedure is a regular feature. These shows reject the idea of doctors as Gods while they remain fascinated with the ethical implications of doctors 'playing God'.

The ability to connect to societal knowledges and anxieties about healthcare, and balance emergency treatment with explorations of personal and professional identity allowed the 1990s hospital dramas to access a wide range of dramatic possibilities. The shows that exploit those possibilities most successfully form the backbone of this book: *ER, Chicago Hope, Cardiac Arrest*, and to a lesser extent, *Gideon's Crossing* (ABC, 2000–01), *Always and Everyone* (ITV, 1999–2000) and *Casualty*. The book does not consider shows that merely incorporate medico-morbid themes and characters such as the use of forensic pathologists in *Silent Witness, Cracker, The X-Files* and *Millennium*. Neither do I consider non-fiction shows such as *Trauma: Life in the ER, Children's Hospital, Code Blue, The Human Body, Body Story* and various doctor, nurse or hospital-based docusoaps. The reason for avoiding hospital-based docusoaps in particular is that they often seem to embody precisely that morbid gaze exhibited by the cameraman in *ER*'s live episode. Such shows raise ethical issues that fictional television avoids since their depicted worlds have the advantage of being under the total control of the creators.

I have also avoided detailed treatment of fictional shows that I consider adjacent to the genre: these include the *Casualty* spin-off *Holby City*, the quasi-sitcom *Scrubs*, medical ethics serial, *Life Support*, and the show centred around mental healthcare, *Psychos*. Many of the findings of this book should be applicable to these shows, however; no doubt the patterning of action and reflection, presentation of multiple stories and themes of compromised romance, training and moral and ethical issues exist in different ways in each of them. If most of my examples and analysis refer to *ER* it is in the recognition that it is an outstanding hospital drama that developed the features of the genre and confirmed that US television understands its television series and serial drama as a form of art.

What are the features of new hospital dramas? The rest of the book constitutes an answer; a definition that is broad enough to encompass the diverse interests of the genre must include the interest in showing the human body – variously injured, wounded, diseased, in distress – a body in ruins, as the stimulus for drama. The genre is primarily concerned with the *immediacy* of trauma and its treatment, rather than long-term disease, sickness or ill health. These television fictions would be unremarkable if all they did was to reflect contemporary concerns and anxieties since, obviously, all creative works are products of their time. The achievement of body trauma television at its best lies in the way that it uses the resonance of an anxious age as the basis for drama that explores the wages of accident, death, injury and disease in a compelling manner. The paradox is that the pleasure and vitality of the drama is dependent on such unpleasant and horrifying subject matter.

Notes

1. Ludwig Wittgenstein, *Philosophical Investigations* (Oxford: Blackwell, 2000, first published 1953), p. 178.
2. *ER*, 'Ambush', season 4, episode 1 (1997).
3. As the image approaches its closest position to the face it loses focus momentarily. Although this episode was broadcast live, the documentary crew featured in it are not transmitting live images, but taping for a later broadcast; this allows Greene to negotiate with the director so that he will offer an interview if they do not show Carter's distress at losing the patient.
4. Interviewed on *Playing Doctor* (BBC, 1996).
5. *Dr Kildare*, 'A Life for a Life' (1965).
6. Anne Karpf, *Doctoring the Media* (London: Routledge, 1988), p. 191.
7. The band that exemplified the grunge identity, Nirvana, was occasionally referenced in the *mise en scène* of the show.
8. Michael Fitzpatrick, *The Tyranny of Health: Doctors and the Regulation of Lifestyle* (London: Routledge, 2001), p. 160.
9. Susan Sontag, *Illness as Metaphor*; and, *AIDS and its Metaphors* (London: Penguin Books, 1991), p. 173.
10. Andy Medhurst, 'Still hooked on pulse fiction', *The Sunday Times* (30 April 1995), p. 13.
11. See the accounts of particular medical dramas in Karpf, *Doctoring the Media*, and Joseph Turow, *Playing Doctor: Television, Storytelling and Medical Power* (Oxford: Oxford University Press, 1989).

I

Genre and Context

The introduction sketched the periodisation of television hospital drama in three broad stages: 'paternal' (1950s–mid-1960s), 'conflict' (late 1960s–1980s) and 'apocalyptic' (1990s). These labels are indicative of the content and worldview of those dramas; I want to flesh this out by examining the particular ways in which the change from the 'conflict' dramas to the 'apocalyptic' took place. As noted before, it is not the case that new hospital dramas represented a clean break with earlier instances of the genre but that they inherited many of the concerns, plots and character-types from their predecessors at the same time as they developed different approaches to the treatment of theme,style, pace and characterisation. Hence the new hospital dramas incorporate continuity with earlier and adjacent genres as well as promoting distinct features that set them apart.

M*A*S*H and the absurd

We have already seen that the 1970s sitcom *M*A*S*H* depicted doctors with little or no control over the hostile environment in which they were forced to treat casualties. The hostile working environment was an essential and innovative component in the formula of the show (no doubt earlier medical dramas confronted their doctors with hostile environments, but not routinely[1]), and *M*A*S*H* was important in introducing in sitcom form elements that were central to later shows like *ER*. As Larry Gelbart (co-creator of the TV series) argues, 'Putting *M*A*S*H* as a dot in the centre you could probably draw lines to even current shows which emulate the flippant quality, the pace, the multi-tiered stories.'[2] *M*A*S*H* foregrounded several aspects that were to become essential to new hospital dramas – the hostile setting as a means to explore the relationship between personal and professional lives; the absurd juxtaposition of war with medical treatment; and the figure of the doctor as confused humanist exemplified by the character of Benjamin Franklin 'Hawkeye' Pierce, and a liberal deployment of black humour and gallows laughter.

As Joseph Turow notes in his book *Playing Doctor*, *M*A*S*H* represented an attempt by the television industry to refresh the medical drama form by combining it with the sitcom format.[3] This was never going to be easy to sell to the US networks since wounded soldiers and jokes told during the process of stitching them up created an uneasy position for the viewer to occupy, one that was not resolved by using the laugh track to cue a response at 'appropriate' moments.[4] Although there were industry worries that the public would not stomach the juxtaposition of comedy and surgery, the show went on to become one of the most successful television series of all time. The creators of the TV show, Larry Gelbart and Gene Reynolds, had never worked on a medical show before and their primary research came from viewing other television medical shows, as well as interviewing doctors who had worked in Vietnam.[5] As Turow points out the decision to set the characters in a historical war zone had significant consequences in the development of the genre:

> It ... drastically reversed the traditional approach of doctor shows to their patients and their settings. Previous programs, from Medic through Marcus Welby had focused on the impact (usually positive) of the doctors on their patients and social environment. M*A*S*H, by contrast, centered on the impact (usually negative) of the patients and the environment on the physicians.[6]

The difficulties in convincing the networks to take the material have a clear thematic analogue in the show itself. In common with earlier medical shows where bureaucratic 'pencil pushers' would often hassle the medical staff, the M*A*S*H unit has to combat the administrative absurdity of 'I-Corps', the military command which was, as many have argued, an analogue to the network itself.[7] The show was self-consciously about exploring the boundaries between comedy and drama so much so that one network executive complained to Alan Alda (Hawkeye) about a particular episode where a central character dies – 'What is this? A situation tragedy?'[8] M*A*S*H's discovery was that the absurd could function politically and comedically at the same time within the sitcom form.

M*A*S*H's juxtaposition of comedy, surgical treatment and war – and, more importantly, its attitude to that juxtaposition – aligned it with literature of the absurd such as Joseph Heller's Catch-22 (1961) and the work of Camus and Beckett. The theme for the show 'Suicide is Painless' was indicative of the 'desperate edge' to the comedic mode of address where irony would be a central theme.[9] As Gene Reynolds noted:

> What the [M*A*S*H doctors] are doing is absurd, it's futile ... They're in a middle of a war where everything is designed to destroy, to tear bodies up, to

maim, to kill. They're in the business of putting these bodies back together again, only to have them sent back – sort of like recycling people – which becomes like shoving a rock up a hill only to have it roll down.[10]

This is a variation on the situation depicted in *Catch-22* where the protagonists' desire to get out of a situation condemns them to remain trapped within it. As Andrew Calcutt points out in his critique of the political limitations of pop culture, the absurd or ironic response often entails a resignation to the fact that human activity is limited in the face of forces it cannot influence:

> In *Catch-22* there is no escape from the paradox that to report one's own insanity is
> itself the action of a sane man. By the same token, there is no let-out from war,
> and, by implication, the destruction of our humanity. All the protagonist can do to
> reassert his humanity is to appreciate the absurdity of the situation.[11]

M*A*S*H is significant because of the way in which it develops the Hawkeye character in relation to the absurd. After Gelbart's departure Alan Alda began to exert increasing influence on the direction and tone of the show. As a result Hawkeye became more introspective and the impact of feminism clearly mellowed his earlier Lothario instincts. By the later seasons Hawkeye is a banjaxed humanist trying to do good in an absurd world where the odds are stacked against him. In a speech given to the Columbia University's College of Physicians and Surgeons in 1979, Alda commented on Hawkeye:

> He's not a magician who can come up with an instant cure for a rare disease
> without sweating and ruining his make-up. He knows he might fail. Not a god, he
> walks gingerly on the edge of disaster – alive to his own mortality.[12]

David Marc and John Caldwell both note the importance of *M*A*S*H* in the development of television fiction towards more self-conscious, authored and philosophising modes. The series experimented with formal innovation such as black and white newsreel, and the occasional suspension of the laugh-track (episodes that Caldwell calls 'Emmy bait'). In its later years the Alda/Hawkeye figure was frequently positioned as a self-reflexive narrator. According to Caldwell:

> By the middle years of the series Alan Alda had assumed control from Larry
> Gelbart as the show's creative force. Alda eventually became the only person to
> win Emmys for acting, writing and directing. This publicised aura enabled the
> quality ensemble associated with the series to pursue tactics that became hallmarks

of postmodernist television in the 1980s: including the masquerade of style, pastiche and extreme self-consciousness about the artifice of television.[13]

M*A*S*H uses the longevity, continuity and memory of the series form to explore questions of a nation's memory and understanding of itself, and this is exemplified by the transition of Alda's character from that of a womanising joker – a child of the 1960s – to a mode of reflective introversion. As David Marc puts it: 'Interpersonal relationships gradually shoved American foreign policy issues to the textual margins; a sixties revisionist history of the fifties gave way to a seventies revisionist history of the sixties.'[14] It is significant that Marc invokes Norman Mailer's 1959 essay 'The White Negro' in his description of Hawkeye as a sitcom frontiersman in a post-atomic bomb, post-Holocaust world. Mailer's essay seeks an appropriate response to an absurd world and finds it in the adoption of a psychopathic persona. As Calcutt argues, Mailer's adoption of the psychopathic personality as a plausible response to the absurdity of modern life was indicative of the increasing fashionable embrace of madness as a form of insight, and aesthetic posture.[15] It is also evident in the development of the psychology of television characters in long-running series, notably Hawkeye himself who, in the final episode of *M*A*S*H* undergoes psychotherapy where he discovers he is indirectly responsible for the death of an infant refugee. In his essay on television, Stanley Cavell also refers to 'The White Negro' in an attempt to understand the 'fear' of television, a fear he locates as a response to the increasing uninhabitability of the world.[16] The new hospital dramas partake of this fear too in their depictions of a world of violence, with disease and injury invading the hospital corridor, a world where Hobbes's *bellum omnium contra omnes* (the war of all against all) reigns.

By the 1980s Hawkeye's existential angst had been dispersed among the ensemble cast of *St Elsewhere*. *St Elsewhere* exploited the fact that the cast allowed viewer identification, sympathy and alignment to be variously dispersed between characters, so we share 'multi-dimensional involvement'.[17] As in *M*A*S*H*, *St Elsewhere*'s setting in a depressed urban environment at a Boston teaching hospital, St Eligius, was largely a hostile one. Like the new hospital dramas it used multiple storylines and a distinctive visual style. *St Elsewhere* was made by MTM Enterprises who had produced the innovative *Hill Street Blues* for NBC in 1981; the former incorporated much of the gritty realist house style associated with the latter. MTM employed a young staff (all in their early thirties) who were interested in taking risks and exploring the traditions of the genre. *St Elsewhere*'s creator, Josh Brand, admitted that his intention was to recreate the hospital genre in a realistic way:

I'm not a guy who's familiar with television, and I wasn't familiar with other television medical shows. I mean, I remember vaguely *Ben Casey* and *Kildare*, and though I never watched *Marcus Welby* I knew what kind of guy he was. And that always seemed to me very silly. And you know I remember when we first did [*St Elsewhere*] and were meeting with the press, I said, 'I don't know about you, but I never had a doctor come to my door and ask how I'm feeling today.'[18]

In Brand's show the doctors behaved badly, making jokes and talking crudely about patients. Instead of being distinct from it, the patients are rendered as another part of the hostile environment. The show connected with fashionable ideas of 'yuppie angst' and 'yuppie diseases' that began to circulate in the 1980s, and also with the growing morbidity of the middle class and their – often displaced – fears of the disease- and violence-spreading lower classes. As Turow points out:

In fact it was the patients who made up a large part of what made life in a *St Elsewhere* episode tough for the doctors and nurses. Adopting the hero-as-victim perspective implicit in *M*A*S*H* and *Hill Street Blues*, *St Elsewhere* went further than any previous doctor series in portraying patients as part of a threatening, problem-causing environment for doctors. Previous doctor dramas typically had physicians acting as catalysts who helped patients explore (and often resolve) their emotional and physical difficulties. Patients in *St Elsewhere*, by contrast, were more often the cause of wide-ranging personal problems for the physicians responsible for dealing with them.[19]

Questions of career, personal worth, spiritual direction and other introspective matters were the main content of the shows. Its realism was based less on the accurate portrayal of a hospital than the detailing of personal psychologies and interpersonal conflict. *St Elsewhere* provided a model for character development in the new hospital dramas and also was successful in translating an actual war setting to a figurative/psychological one: doctors were at war with the hospital administration, their patients and themselves. Joseph Turow identifies this change and new emphasis taking place in the 1970s where there was a

shift from an anthology-style focus on problems of the patients to a greater concern with the personal and professional difficulties of the medical people themselves [creating] an unusual pessimism about the ability of physicians to carry out their mandate to provide virtually unlimited resources for medical care.[20]

The focus on pessimism and the limits of finite resources for healthcare signalled the growing abandonment of 'reassurance' as a command address to the audience with the implication that they would no longer accept it as a convincing view of the world.

Casualty and the war zone

The persistent use of the 'war zone' to describe the hospital setting as well as the troubled relationships between doctors and the patients (indeed the routine use of 'incoming' to describe their imminent arrival) or phrases such as 'the front line' to describe the work of medical staff signals the way that the military metaphors were becoming routinely presented in television hospital dramas as indicative of a healthcare service under siege. Figuring the hospital as either a war zone in itself or adjacent to one, just outside the double swing doors, was firmly established as a generic feature of hospital dramas by the mid-1980s. The UK hospital drama Casualty is important here because the show tended to understand itself as part of a campaign against UK government cuts to the health service.

Casualty started out as 'The Front Line' and the creators Jeremy Brock and Paul Unwin initially wanted the staff in the ward to wear combat fatigues. The first page of the blueprint for the series read: 'In 1945 a dream was born in the National Health Service. In 1985 that dream is in tatters.'[21] Unwin remembers that '... there was a lot of concern about the running down of the National Health Service then. We wanted to do a campaigning programme with that feeling of being on the ground, in the thick of it.'[22] Brock and Unwin also cite M*A*S*H as an influence:

> [We were] trying to create a situation that was almost like a war in that
> department. When we first thought of the idea we were going to have the
> characters crash through the doors and that was the beginning of the story, and it
> was very M*A*S*H-like in that way. Bang! – and they came through. We were
> quickly told that wasn't going to be possible and we had to reduce the idea down.
> Like we had to get them out of army fatigues because it simply didn't happen.[23]

The BBC – itself on the receiving end of aggressive government criticism during the 1980s – approved their idea in 1985. It was apparent that the show would seek to demystify hospital care and undermine any residual glamour:

> [the hospital 'Holby City'] would be staffed by unglamorous people. Into it would
> flock the careless, the careworn, the drunk, the addicted, the crushed, the bashed,
> the mad and the bad. It would not be a place of quiet sanctuary and respect. It
> would be an extension of the street, a rough street at that, in which medical

miracles were rare and damage limitation was often the best that could be achieved. Its stories and style would upset politicians, irritate health workers and open wounds in the minds of some of its audience.[24]

According to Hilary Kingsley *Casualty*'s success lay in the blending of elements of the medical drama genre with soap, documentary and political report, as well as its relatively novel depiction of toxic patients:

> The patients weren't pets, any of them. They included a baby-snatcher, a haemophiliac with a slit wrist refusing treatment because of the Aids panic; a homeless old tramp with shingles; a wife basher and child abuser; an Indian boy who suffered alcohol poisoning; football supporters who stabbed a policeman; junkies attempting suicide ...[25]

The war of all against all indeed. What was missing, at any sustained level, was the undercurrent of existential agony and sense of the absurd that was an essential feature of *M*A*S*H* and *St Elsewhere*. Instead, *Casualty*'s agonising was directed at the impact of welfare cuts and the stupidity of introducing free market principles into a healthcare system. Where the US shows used the setting to tie issues of psychological exploration with modernity itself, *Casualty* explored ideas at the level of social and policy-oriented issues which were nationally specific. Its characters were far more likely to exemplify or represent aspects of social movements or folk devils energised by media news stories and as such they were rather thinly psychologised. A lot of what was wrong in the *Casualty* ward originated in financial shortages resulting in threats to axe the night shift because of under-funding, a constant lack of beds and staff, and limited equipment. It was alleged at the time that some scripts were written by supporters of far Left groups in the UK and it was well known that members of cast, particularly Derek Thompson (Charlie Fairhead), were outspoken critics of welfare cuts. Despite its apparent critical edge, the show's alignment was emphatically with the medical staff on the casualty night shift rather than with the patients, in sharp contrast to Dennis Potter's *The Singing Detective* (also shown in 1986 on the BBC), which was bitterly critical of the way in which patients were routinely infantilised by the medical profession.

Casualty then was strongly bound to contemporary issues in UK healthcare and part of its appeal was its integration of medico-political news stories into its drama. As former head of BBC drama, Mal Young, noted,

> *Casualty* has succeeded because every year it has evolved and moved on. Look at early programmes, or even those just two or three years old and they seem dated.

The whole point of the series, I feel, is that each series should be 'of the moment'.[26]

What sets *Casualty* apart from other hospital dramas is its insistence on sketching the lives of its patients before they become sick or injured so that we know something about them. Other hospital shows do this intermittently but in *Casualty* it is a routine feature. The background sketches present the potential patients in the context of ordinary events and objects such as car journeys, kitchen appliances and children playing happily; this makes it a loaded *mise en scène* that is cast with the grim anticipation of the accident that will produce a serious injury. The hostile setting is in some ways extended from the emergency ward and into potentially dangerous landscapes of the domestic and everyday. This is not a narrative procedure that was aped by new hospital dramas probablybecause it limits the flexibility of narrative design and can reduce viewer involvement to the game of 'spot the victim'.[27] Nevertheless, the achievement of *Casualty* was to bring into mainstream television a thoroughly political oppositional sensibility that raised the stakes of what was being depicted in the narrative worlds of medical dramas. This was bound up with the development of its own generic peculiarities (the sketches) and a consistent desire to represent injury and illness with realistic special effects make-up. With its sense of social responsibility and commitment to realism *Casualty* can be seen as a rather traditional example of public service television broadcasting. But *Casualty* proved to be adaptable beyond the time when public service broadcasting had become obsolete in policy and practice in British television; in part this was because it responded to the challenges of US hospital dramas in the mid-1990s. Despite significant differences with *Casualty* (see Chapter 3), *Cardiac Arrest* maintained and sharpened that sense of the hospital as war zone and the function of hospital dramas as somehow to demystify the medical profession at the same time as 'raising awareness' of pressing political issues relating to healthcare provision. In this sense both held on to a rather 'public service broadcasting' ideal in their conception of the public sphere.

ER and Chicago Hope

The premiere of *ER* and *Chicago Hope* in 1994 marks the beginning of the new hospital dramas as a popular mainstream product (although the UK's *Cardiac Arrest* began earlier it was less well known and did not achieve the same critical praise: *ER* was nominated for seventeen Emmys in 1996, *Chicago Hope* for fifteen). *ER* began as a film script written in 1974 by former doctor Michael Crichton but rejected by Hollywood at that time. It remained unmade for some twenty years before Crichton teamed up with Steven Spielberg, who was then adapting Crichton's novel *Jurassic Park* for the big screen. They adapted the script as a TV pilot and series format.[28]

Crichton was a badge of distinction at a time when many of his best-selling novels were being transformed into Hollywood blockbusters, some made by that other badge of distinction, Steven Spielberg. *ER* also recruited quality television veterans, notably John Wells who was executive producer on *China Beach* (ABC, 1988–91) and later *The West Wing* (NBC,1999–). Wells describes Crichton's script as particularly unusual:

> One of the chief complaints about the script was that you didn't know who you were supposed to care about … that there wasn't a beginning, middle and end – it was really just a series of small scenes. It had multiple storylines, and many stories that were just one beat and didn't go anywhere else. There was very little standard dramatic through line. *ER* was like a pointillist painting … looking closely at the bits and pieces of scenes, they seemed not to make sense. But when you stepped back, they added up to an emotional tapestry that was very moving.[29]

Crichton's script formed the basis of the pilot episode but subsequent episodes and seasons were crafted under Wells's creative control. Wells retained Crichton's emphases on the quality that *ER* has subsequently become famous for – its speed. As Crichton says, 'Pace was vital as I knew from my own experience. I was looking for speed and raw feel.'[30] The stylish speed and fluidity of *ER*'s camerawork was clearly intended to be expressive of the contemporary world as well as the emergency room, a world that was seen as risky, uncertain and dangerous.

Setting *ER* in a hostile environment – the hospital is the cash-strapped 'County General' servicing inner-city Chicago patients – made it distinct from *Chicago Hope*, which was set in a wealthy research hospital with the best surgeons in the world. *ER*'s cast was younger and reflected a broad ethnic and gender scale, but there was also a different kind of seriousness in each. *Chicago Hope*, like other David E. Kelley shows, tended to be quirky, comic and often wearing its sensitivity and quirkiness on its sleeve. *ER* had a darker sense of the hostile outside world that was only occasionally mollified with humour. Nevertheless, *ER* won the battle of the ratings and has remained consistently rated at the top or near in the ratings compared to its one-time rival, something satirised in the following exchange between two guests on *The Larry Sanders Show* (HBO, 1992–8):

Mandy Patinkin (Dr Geiger in Chicago Hope*):* Your show is broader, ours is more character-driven, and it deals with sensitive issues.

Noah Wyle (Dr Carter in ER*):* Nobody watches your show.
Mandy Patinkin: I don't watch our fuckin' show.[31]

While *Chicago Hope* tended to concentrate more on gory body horror and complex legal matters involving the custody of body parts, *ER* pushed the generic envelope in a different direction by concentrating its attention on the medical staff and using their patients as method for reflecting back onto the characters issues of procedure, ethics and personal morality. As Crichton claimed:

> I wanted to write something that was based in reality … Something that would have a fast pace and treat medicine in a realistic way. The screenplay was very unusual. It was very focused on the doctors, not the patients – the patients came and went. People yelled paragraphs of drug dosages at each other. It was very technical, almost a quasi-documentary. But what interested me was breaking standard dramatic structure. I understood that's what the screenplay did, but I always felt that it was compulsively watchable.[32]

What is acknowledged as 'realistic' changes, of course, as television genres and the worlds they depict change. For some, *ER*'s claim to realism was to be found in its overall narrative tone in the way it offered disillusionment rather than reassurance. This meant that it articulated an apocalyptic sensibility that involved the acknowledgment of failure and being 'at the end of things'. For example, this gloomy description of *ER* was intended as high praise: '[t]he programme is as much about disillusionment as miracle surgery. It often ends on a downbeat, reflective note about personal and medical failures as well as the larger failures of American society.'[33] Alongside speed and spectacle the narrativising of failure and disillusionment rather than reassurance became a central characteristic of new hospital dramas, and the development of the genre reflects this changing process. Was this shift a product of cultural changes in attitudes and values or an early aesthetic anticipation of a growing cultural pessimism? To what extent was the genre itself acknowledging its own need for renewal?

Generic self-awareness in the new hospital dramas
In 1996 the BBC showed 'Docs on the Box' – 'an evening of programmes celebrating television doctors, with a line-up of medical dramas from past and present'. The selection included episodes of *Casualty*, *Dr Finlay's Casebook*, *Dr Kildare*, *M*A*S*H* and a documentary called *Playing Doctor* where doctors, producers, writers and actors reflected upon the development of the medical dramas they helped to create in Britain and the US. The timing of the theme night signalled the recognition of the proliferation of medical dramas during the

The paternal relationship: Kildare (Richard Chamberlain) administers wisdom as Gillespie (Raymond Massey) looks on in *Dr Kildare*

mid-1990s that was beginning to rival the crime fiction genre. Three years before, the BBC showed a 'Cops on the Box' evening that included a similar mixture of archival material and contemporary comment. By the mid-1990s the tide seemed to be changing towards dramatising worlds where medical pathology rather than law and order provided the dominant dramatic themes.[34] As Charlotte Brunsdon notes,

> Arguably, the dynamic genre of the 1990s is the medical drama. There is at the same time a move towards the medicalisation of crime within the crime series, with the focus moving away from the police as solvers of riddles to pathologists ... and criminal psychologists.[35]

Playing Doctor presents generic development as a product of the programme-makers' desire to depict medicine with greater realism and an increasing willingness to handle controversial topics. While that trend was an undeniable feature of nearly all television genres during that period, what was different in the 1990s was the emergence of a generation of creative personnel who had grown up with a built-in awareness of television genre. The writers and actors interviewed in *Playing Doctor* demonstrate a shrewd knowledge of the way in which *St Elsewhere*, *M*A*S*H* and *Dr Kildare* depicted the medical practice so that they see themselves as inhabiting and contributing to a pre-existing tradition. For example, Jed Mercurio, creator and writer of *Cardiac Arrest* says:

> I watched a lot of medical programmes towards the end of when I was in school because I was developing an interest in medicine ... the ones I watched were *Casualty* and *St Elsewhere* and programmes like that, and that's how I derived my opinion of what being a doctor would be like. You know, television made me choose that as a job ... You watch TV and you see these guys have a really good

time and you think, Oh wow I'll be a doctor, it must be brilliant ... Then you do the job and you realise it's a piece of crap and you think, right I'm going to make a television programme that tells the truth. So that loads of people watch mine and then go, 'I'm not going to be a doctor'.[36]

Mercurio's comments illustrate the way in which television genres can develop in response to themselves, and the very existence of *Playing Doctor* illustrates that television's institutions were themselves reflecting on their history. Being able to understand and compare generic histories is only possible when television has a commodity form, where examples of its programmes are retrievable, able to be repeated – say from the early 1950s onwards. But the 'televisual memory' also inheres in individuals, those who grew up watching television – made at an early stage by those who did not – and who now make television programmes, write them, act in them, watch them. If we date television's widespread dispersal and availability to the early to mid-1950s, then it seems likely that those people who reached positions of creative influence in television during the 1980s and 90s probably were among the first generation to grow up watching television as a regular leisure activity. For these generations television is no longer a new medium, it has a tradition, a past, and a history that is internalised by programmes, their creators and their audience. Karen Lury has usefully described the consequences of generational differences in viewing biographies for our understanding of television performance. (Not only 'viewing biographies': Charlotte Brunsdon has noted how *Inspector Morse* acknowledges its lead actor's previous career starring in *The Sweeney*.)[37] Hence 'television' – reified as the sum of those creating and watching its programmes – understands its own genres in relation to past and present. It is not surprising that new generic forms seem very knowing about their place in a tradition and in some cases they may constitute a study of the possibilities of the genre itself. As Steve Bailey notes in his examination of 'professional television',

the kind of struggle dramatised within the narrative structures of these programs and exploding out into a variety of discourses, including those of the specific production of the same programs, has a long history within the internal industrial and external – governmental, critical, and so on – rhetorics surrounding television.[38]

In the 'external' sphere, television critics and scholars similarly come to television with a built-in experiential knowledge of those generic traditions.[39] Andy Medhurst identifies different traditions within the medical drama that are emphasised in various programmes: the doctor-nurse relationship (*General*

Hospital, The Young Doctors); the infallible hero (*Dr Kildare, Marcus Welby MD*); placing the doctor in a tight-knit community (*Dr Finlay's Casebook, Peak Practice*); the comic potential of bodies (*Doctor in the House*); what he calls 'social democratic activism' (*Angels, Casualty, St Elsewhere*). He describes specific instances of generic inheritance and appropriation ('*Cardiac Arrest* is *M*A*S*H* in another combat zone, transposed from the Korean War to the battle of Bottomley'), and economic and national differences within the genre, between the 'big-budget soaps' such as *ER* and *Chicago Hope* that offer 'a strong streak of utopianism' and the sour 'Brit grit' of *Cardiac Arrest*.[40] Medhurst's account stresses the continuities within the genre and tends to see them as cyclic rather than developing. My account focuses more on the conscious creative innovation as a feature of a developing genre. In Lars von Trier's mini-series *The Kingdom* – first screened in 1994 along with *ER, Cardiac Arrest* and *Chicago Hope* – the very formation of the new hospital drama genre seems to be under examination. Its juxtaposition of horror, soap and the uncanny enable it to create a setting and a discursive address that seems to undermine the claims of rationalist medical science that the other hospital dramas cling onto even in the face of decline and despair. (One might say that the apocalyptic tone of many of them is precisely mourning the decay of rationalism in contemporary culture.)

There are three main aspects of that development in the new hospital dramas: the foregrounding of body trauma as spectacle, the intensification of the genre's melodramatic dimensions and the exploitation of the narrative adaptability of the long- running serialised-series form. I consider the first aspect in the next chapter; the next section considers the significance of setting and form in relation to melodrama.

Melodrama, setting and serial form

The shift from a reassuring address to the pessimistic, disillusioned worlds of the new hospital dramas can be understood as a shift towards medicalised melodrama. Deborah Thomas argues that melodramatic worlds in movies are characterised by danger, repression, displacement, hierarchical power and malign fate. Traditionally the melodramatic has been understood in relation to a hostile world of fate, God, the Devil or sheer malice. In our contemporary culture the 'hidden forces' are pathogens, potential links between disease and lifestyle choices, hidden genetic destinies. As the Calvinists led thrifty, virtuous lives as proof they were chosen, the body-harrowed live with the burden that they will find salvation only through the dedicated monitoring of their inevitable decay. In Thomas's schema comedic worlds offer the possibility of change and transformation, something that these worlds and the characters in them welcome. But melodramatic worlds are hostile, malevolent and often ruled by malign fate.[41] This seems an apt description of life as it was perceived in the West in the 1990s and beyond. As Michael Fitzpatrick argues, 'change in the modern world no longer appears to be the outcome of conscious human direction or purpose – it appears as the unpredictable outcome of the random, chaotic actions of diverse, isolated individuals and uncontrollable social (and natural) forces.'[42] The new hospital dramas routinely dramatise moments of 'body-crisis' that also articulate a sense of the world out of control and in this way reinforce and nurture a sense of powerlessness. It is the nature of television art to articulate, anticipate and aestheticise the changing flow of the world's feelings, values, sensibilities and attitudes. John Ellis calls this 'working through':

> Television can be seen as a vast mechanism for processing the material of the witnessed world into more narrativised, explained forms. The term 'working through' is drawn deliberately from psychoanalysis where it describes the process whereby material is continually worried over until it is exhausted.[43]

I would go further than Ellis, who tends to fix television as a kind of 'relay' that mechanistically processes pre-existing material: in some ways I would argue television can anticipate and articulate quite amorphous trends, feelings and attitudes that only emerge concretely later on. In juxtaposing cultural context with the texts of the new hospital dramas I hope to indicate how that process takes place. Television's serialised-serial form allows it to articulate these sensibilities, anxieties and other dramatic feelings in concrete dramatic forms. Clearly, however, the issue of the relations between society and its aesthetic products is considerable – one thinks first of all of the work of Siegfried Kracauer, Richard Dyer and Raymond Williams, all of whom are very successful in giving words to historically amorphous feelings and sensibilities.[44] To a great extent a similar project concerning television serial drama remains to be done.

Hospital dramas are the ideal genre in which to dramatise the contemporary world's melodramatic sensibilities. Instead of the traditional melodrama's use of the home as the stage for the expression of feeling, new hospital dramas relocate many of the traditional melodramatic concerns to their institutional stage. It is often where many of the characters feel most 'at home'. The hospital setting is a place seemingly set apart from this hostile world and regularly invaded by the wages of its malevolence. Although one could make the distinction between those shows set primarily in the part of the hospital used for treating emergency cases (ER, Casualty, Always and Everyone) and those that offer a wider range of spaces and medical cases (Chicago Hope, Gideon's Crossing, Cardiac Arrest), all of the shows represent acute emergency cases, 'difficult' patients and a variety of domestic settings as well; the issue is one of emphasis rather than limitation.

Although *Cardiac Arrest* is nominally set in a hospital ward occupied by a variety of patients, most of what we see involves the treatment of acute emergencies, and in this respect it has more in common with *ER* than with *Chicago Hope*.

The settings are urban places of work, often tied to a particular city (Chicago in the case of *ER* and *Chicago Hope*, London in *Casualty*), and the foregrounding of the workplace allows the shows to focus attention on medical practice and the tensions, romance and friendship between the central characters. As such they also belong to a wider category, the workplace drama where the setting is a familiar and developing space. As Thomas Schatz argues,

> The workplace in these series ultimately emerges as a character unto itself, and one, which is both harrowing and oddly inspiring to those who work there. For the characters in *ER* and *NYPD Blue* and the other ensemble workplace dramas, soul searching comes with the territory and they know the territory all too well. They are acutely aware not only of their own limitations and failings but of the inadequacies of their own professions to cure the ills of the modern world. Still, they maintain their commitment to one another and to a professional code which is the very life-blood of the workplace they share.[45]

Steve Bailey takes this further and argues that shows like *ER* are part of a 'super genre' of 'professional' television which inherits the neo-liberalism of the 1970s Norman Lear sitcom and *M*A*S*H*, together with a

> similar tendency to engage particularly provocative issues of contemporary concern (from *Maude*'s abortion to *L.A. Law*'s lesbian kiss to *ER*'s explorations of HMO care) and in the continual emphasis on a common struggle by major characters to 'do the right thing' in a difficult situation.[46]

The acknowledgment of professional limitations is built into the new hospital dramas in a way which was less intense in earlier instances of the medical drama. On the one hand they depict extremes of human suffering and injury, something that necessarily encourages viewer proximity. On the other hand this suffering is treated by a group of familiar characters who we have come to know and align ourselves with. These are doctors and nurses who may have little sympathy for their patients, or may just be tired, bothered by other distractions and so on. This results in the uncomfortable comic moments where doctors and surgeons joke about their dying patients, sing during cardiac surgery (*Chicago Hope*, *passim*), or appear amused by the over-anxiety of their patients. Take Claire Maitland's approach in *Cardiac Arrest* to a bewildered patient who is brought in suffering from chest pains:

I suspect the cause of your pain is a tear in the big artery coming out of your heart. We're going to lower your blood pressure and scan your chest. You may require surgery. If the aorta continues to tear you may die of it. Any questions, queries, comments or worries? *[Patient shakes head]* My kind of patient!

The dialogue is delivered in close-up before a quick pan briefly reveals the patient's shocked shaking of his head (he's wearing an oxygen mask), then whips back to Claire as she delivers the punch-line. The proximity of 'you may die' with the cheery 'My kind of patient!' is an obvious attempt at black humour, as is the inclusion of the euphemistic 'worries' as the final item on the diagnostic checklist. We enjoy Claire's directness as a welcome relief from the emotive caring of 'good' television doctors who take their patient's feelings into account when delivering bad news but this is tempered by the recognition that news of our imminent death may well be just one more diagnosis in the working day of a busy doctor, which is the point of the scene. In other words, the proximity of patients suffering mediated through the familiar characters of doctors and nurses invites the audience to adopt complex viewing positions in relation to what they are shown.

Previously, hospital dramas used instances of injury and illness as a means to uncover personal crises which the healthcare staff can manage: the medical team does more than simply solve the immediate injury or disease – their other function is to resolve or clarify the patient's moral problems. This is a recurrent feature of more traditional medical dramas such as *Casualty*, where the medical staff consistently intervene in the personal problems and moral dilemmas of their patients (Should the gay priest come out? Can the loving wife admit that her husband beats her? And so on). It is often acknowledged that the traditional medical genre is not simply about the spectacle of injury but the treatment of social ills, the spectacle of the social body made well morally. Some critics have understood this as an appropriation, by the medical dramas, of the practice of the Christian church, dispensing moral healing to their sick congregations. According to Steven Poole, 'This ... is the consistent argument of *Casualty*: that disease and injury are not accidents but the wages of social disharmony.'[47] Arguing that 'hospitals to some degree are the churches of modernity' Poole suggests that while television's medical priesthood offer bedside epiphanies, and hospitals as places of redemption and salvation, their chief attraction is in dramatising the loss of individual responsibility:

Medical drama shows us only the sedated mind freed from the demands of the body, a luxurious state in which the burden of personhood is entrusted to another. (A patient, after all is the opposite of an agent.) In an age of libertarian politics, medical drama temptingly says: 'Forget the existential fear of infinite choice and the demands of personal conscience; here is a blissful dream of absolute irresponsibility.'[48]

Melodramatic issues are articulated within a dramatic setting where issues of responsibility for the body and its mortality are routinely foregrounded. Hospital dramas can explore these issues at length because of their television form – continuous dramatic serials that may run for many years. This is clearly a larger category of television fiction, a 'serialised-series' where some narratives continue across episodes and some are introduced and resolved within a single episode. This allows a flexible narrative approach so that particular episodes might concentrate on a single character's problems, and other episodes might weave together four or five narrative strands. Unlike the mini-series, where episodes are often numbered as parts of a whole, the continuous serial offers variously weak and strong senses of continuity across episodes. A story may continue across three or more episodes in a season of twenty-two or a story introduced in the early episodes may be 'reactivated' and further developed later on in the season. Each episode has a 'memory' of what came before, so that character development and other story arcs maintain as much coherence as possible. Story arcs come to resolution and closure, even as the serial continues to continue. This is not a unique aspect of hospital dramas, of course, since shows like *The West Wing*, *The Sopranos* and *The X-Files* also share this flexible approach.[49] What is crucial about this form is that it exists in constant tension between the necessity of character development and the requirement that the formula of the show is not distorted to the extent it becomes a different show altogether. Some episodes are rather like 'holidays' away from generic normality, and focus almost exclusively on one or two characters in a location outside the hospital setting. For example, in *ER* two doctors travel to the Californian desert; another episode concentrates on one character, Nurse Hathaway, seen in her house and going shopping; *Casualty* sent two of its doctors to Australia in one episode. While these excursions offer the novelty of different and sometimes exotic locations, the characters 'take the genre with them' and frequently end up treating medical emergencies (so Hathaway's 'holiday' becomes an emergency when she is taken hostage in a corner shop and has to improvise medical care in order to treat the wounded).

Early hospital dramas like *Dr Kildare* and *Marcus Welby* sought to establish their differences from each other, but generic change was often a product of external forces. Both shows introduced more attention to the regular characters and their personal lives, and this gradually transformed the anthology format of the shows (where each weekly episode had a self-contained narrative which the continuing characters dealt with) to that which has a stronger serial element (where stories would continue from week to week, nearly always attached to continuing characters). There were industrial reasons for this change: the success of *Peyton Place* (ABC) in the 1964–5 season, a soap-serial with strong emphasis on the emotional dimensions of its characters' lives, convinced the networks to introduce a running plot alongside the episode-specific anthology plot. The running plot was invariably a romantic one:

> Weaving the two plots together week after week for the next two seasons became a hassle. The writers and on-line producers found themselves breaking many of Jim Moser's original rules about keeping the central characters' pasts a mystery and dealing foremost with a realistic medical story so as not to make it 'soapy.'[50]

Compare this to the ease with which the new hospital dramas routinely weave five or more storylines into one episode and integrate this with continuing issues connected with character development. By the 1990s the hybrid serialised-series became the standard form of all major medical dramas. This combined the advantage of the serial – the development of a narrative and character in depth over weeks – with that of the episodic series – its regular difference and newness.

As the characters develop so too does the familiarity of the writer, actors and directors with the emerging shape of the show. As *ER* writer and producer Carol Flint points out long-running TV series can take on a creative life of their own:

> …the relationship between actors and writers on an episodic show – and especially a long-running one, is uniquely creative. I'm not close friends with any of our actors on *ER*, but I'm intimate with them as artists in a way that perhaps would surprise some of them. When you're writing episodic drama, your stories develop and derive as much from what you witness as you watch the actors in the dailies, as from your own interests and impulses. You write with the voices of these characters, portrayed by these actors, in your head. I don't think I could be happy writing on an episodic show where the actors didn't excite me and inspire me. From a professional and artistic point of view (and with all the dysfunctional possibilities included) writers and actors in episodic drama do become a family.[51]

The serialised-series form also allows structures of anticipation to be established – we live with the characters and their stories over an extended period. This has important consequences for our critical appraisal. On the one hand it allows the in-depth exploration of a character deepening our understanding over time and allowing the show to respond and revise its own characterisations. It also permits 'shorthand' so that characters are 'loaded' with our previous knowledge of them which gives them a dramatic history and weight that would take much longer to establish in a feature film form.

On the other hand, the fact that a character has a past that we know, and that we have seen developed and changed can limit the opportunities available for further change. There is often a sense, around seasons two or three of a show, that all that can be revealed of a character has been done and the writers are confronted with the problem of how to change their character without sabotaging a successful formula. The solution is often to place characters in a kind of behavioural 'loop' – akin to an endless Greek tragedy – where they are forced to revisit similar situations again and again.

Take for example, an early season one episode of *ER*, 'Blizzard'[52]. As usual it weaves particular episode-specific narrative strands over on-going character development so that the contingency of accidental injury is set into relief against our pre-existing knowledge and therefore expectations of the lives of the main characters. The episode takes place in late December and begins by showing a quiet ER with no patients to treat; the medical staff occupy themselves by watching the development of a severe blizzard on the television news, in-between fooling around. The news announces that a massive car accident has taken place and the staff prepare for the arrival of multiple victims. The preparations for the incoming traumas – arranging medical materials, prepping rooms, collecting instruments, plasma, etc. – is overlayed with some bass-rich music that connotes military preparations and (in contrast to the sound), a visual style that adopts a rather dreamlike mixture of floating steadicam and multiple dissolves that depict the ordered preparation for incoming casualties as well as the uncertainty and anxiety of the medical staff. After treating a heavy influx of injured, traumatised and dying patients, the medical staff re-group and the episode ends with them enjoying some festive celebrations, set to a non-diegetic song (a version of 'Have Yourself a Merry Little Christmas').

During the final moments of the episode, and as the song continues, Dr Mark Greene (Anthony Edwards), a central character in the show, leaves the festivities in full swing; he does not say goodbye but surveys the pleasant communal celebrations with a mixture of satisfaction and wistful regret at his taking leave. The final scene presents us with a meeting between Greene and the proud new parents of a baby he helped to deliver (remotely over the telephone); he takes a look at the child, offers his congratulations, we see him watching as they walk away, and then he does, alone, a view rendered with a gradually ascending crane shot. We fade to black and a faint echo of sleigh bells can be heard.

Viewed in isolation the scene and this episode as a whole is sentimental and cliché-ridden. The idea that the horror of a multiple car pile-up can be negated or healed by a party and sing-song or the birth of a new human life is not only tired but here, carrying the weight of the ending, is forced. Add the Christmas setting and the connotations of nativity-as-redemption become hard to bear: this looks like emotional opportunism at its worst. One could defend the scene in terms of realism: the rewards of community, the pleasures in celebrating the season of goodwill are just as likely to be eagerly grasped by medical staff after experiencing that night of horror and death. If the characters had slumped around amid the decorations moaning about 'the horror, the horror' we could legitimately ask what right they had to be medical staff in the first place, since serious multiple injuries – at least in this show – are commonplace; and we might be affronted by the obvious juxtaposition of decoration and despair. We might also welcome the show's consideration of *our* Christmas mood, its desire to leave us with something positive and upbeat. After all, Christmas time is a period when excess and sentimentality are both legitimate and harmless.

I agree that the charge of opportunism is available, but it is important that the emphasis of this ending is on Greene's leaving (he does not stay, dress up as Santa and hand out gifts). He is leaving to join his family who live outside the city. The charge of sentimentality ignores what we already know and what we might anticipate about that character. At the beginning of the season he is picked out as the only major cast member who is married: the marriage is under strain because of his commitment to his job in the ER and his wife's competing desire to establish a legal career in a different state. Previous episodes also signal the strong friendship between Greene and Dr Susan Lewis (Sherry Stringfield) which has clear romantic potential. Greene leaves a party, where we see the community of medical staff in a festive mood, sharing takeaway food, all differences apparently reconciled. Greene's looking back then is not just at the happy new parents, but at a happy marriage, *and* at a community of friends he must regularly leave in order to fulfil his domestic obligations. The show has been careful to construct Greene's relationship to his wife towards the side of obligation rather than satisfied love. This should colour our judgment of that final shot, or at least make our judgment what it has to be, provisional. That my reading is available at all implies that the show can delicately balance the demands of the particular episode with a fidelity to the story arc of Mark's disintegrating marriage, and the overall development of his character. Given our early position in the first season on the rise of that story arc we might speculate that Greene's wistful satisfaction will only be temporary.

It is sometimes useful to imagine, or remember, what it was like to watch an episode for the first time in the face of relative ignorance about what was to come. Such historicist readings can remind us how what are now conventions once appeared fresh and innovative. Going back to this episode several years after first seeing it I was struck both by how familiar the dramatic situations were and how clumsy their treatment appeared. For example we see Doug Ross (George Clooney) performing triage at the ER door, failing in his haste to identify and treat serious cases of what turns out to be a fatal illness. This provides the basis for the subsequent close-up showcasing of his melodrama of regret as he informs the dead man's spouse, 'We did everything we could, but ...', a situation that is by now a routine generic feature. In a way that is the measure of the success of the show since its innovations have since become the standard. Nevertheless, I was impressed by how elegantly Greene and Lewis's potential relationship is insinuated in various moments of friendly dialogue, so that by the second season the accumulation of our desire for the consummation of theirs becomes unbearable. And looking back after eight seasons of ER, it is clear that Mark's 'unravelling' is the beginning of a series of medical and personal catastrophes that he is confronted with and which effectively turn him from caring doctor to potential murderer: his competency is challenged, his wife leaves him, he is beaten up, his authority is undermined, his parents die, and he eventually dies from brain cancer.[53] The nonchalance of that look back at the parents and ER is cruelly paid out, perhaps excessively so.[54] That final image is haunted by the possibilities of his future. ER uses the advantages of the form and the opportunities of the genre to present a sophisticated and nuanced drama. A further advantage of having long-running series that develop and grow is that they can, over the course of their run, connect and respond to changing social and cultural contexts within which they are made. Does this mean that they simply reflect those contexts? Or does it mean as I hinted before that they illustrate and anticipate in their drama particular sensibilities in play at their time of making? To what extent are vague variables such as 'mood' and 'sensibility' traceable over the run of a television series? The next section details some relevant contexts for these questions in relation to the new hospital dramas.

Contexts

> If the nineteenth century gave rise to utopias, the twentieth century spurred anti-utopias. Since the beginning of the century ... the mood has been of collapse and decay.[55]

In 1995 John O'Reilly described the new appetite for a 'virulently voyeuristic' mode of reality TV as a product of unhealthy popular desires: 'we will turn on to anything that just might sate our desire to get up close to real events, raw emotion, and authentic feeling.'[56] According to O'Reilly that feeling was attached to a distinctive embodied hand-held camera style that provided a 'reality effect': 'In life or death situations the panic the camera conveys lets us know just how shaky things really are.'[57] The embodied expressionism of the hand-held image was countered by *ER*'s use of the steadicam that, unlike the 'restless photography' of *NYPD Blue*, 'makes the most extensive use yet, for a television series, of Steadicam's smooth mobility .... a judicious admission of one part of the medium's artificiality'.[58] By the mid-1990s in the UK the inheritance of the new reality TV aesthetic was clear. Mark Lawson argued that *Cardiac Arrest* and *This Life* display 'obvious symptoms of Bochco-envy'.[59] Other critics saw the integration of the reality shows' aesthetics as less an industry response to recession than indicative of the increased voyeuristic appetite among increasingly fragmented television audiences. In relation to hospital drama this was clearly 'unhealthy' in the eyes of many television critics and cultural commentators. Jim Shelley argued that such shows 'inspire our voyeurism' and cited the popularity of reality formats such as *Hospital Watch* (BBC, 1991) and the long-running *Jimmys* (Yorkshire TV, 1987–94). According to Shelley, 'The signs are that television's obsession with illness and our fascination with it have reached fetishistic proportions.'[60] For these critics the central context is the 'real world' where the unhealthy appetites of the viewing population are catered for by television's voyeuristic gaze. One clear context for them was the assumption of an appetite among the television audience that was catered for by television shows: this is a false way of seeing things insofar as television is less a supplier to audience demand than a stimulator of demand and has, at least until recently, set the agenda for programme innovation rather than relying on the audience to somehow transmit their desires to the industry itself. This assumption occludes the creative appetites and ambitions of programme makers to innovate in the genre and improve their television art which is clearly a vital factor in the development of the new hospital shows. However, there is an audience and industry expectation that drama is at least plausible (even if set in fantastic worlds) and at best realistic (even if stylised), which is why many of them seek to connect with contemporary issues.

In her essay on contemporary British crime fiction, Charlotte Brunsdon explores what she calls 'the relevant discursive contexts for the production and consumption of these programmes' – law and order, privatisation and equal opportunities.[61] She goes on to show how these contexts are variously engaged by generic instances. Although Brunsdon is (necessarily) vague about the ways in which discursive contexts relate to the creative practice of making television programmes, her idea has the advantage of being flexible enough to pose interesting questions about text and context without being overwhelmed by thorny issues of mediation. As far as medical drama is concerned there are two relevant contexts that need to be considered: the national provision of healthcare and the growing fascination with and medicalisation of self, society and the body.

National healthcare provision

National healthcare provision is obviously a major context since most hospitals in the genre cater for the general public. UK and US healthcare contexts differ of course (with the latter more dependent on Health Maintenance Organisations [HMOs], and private insurance); I want to begin by considering the UK's National Health Service (NHS).

The NHS has significant cultural and political resonance in the UK. Established by the Labour government in 1948 the NHS was set up under the slogan 'universal healthcare according to need'. Soon after, fees for medicines and dental care were introduced and by the 1970s the Labour government were proposing significant cuts in NHS funding. Nevertheless the NHS acquired symbolic status as the institution where capitalism was subordinated to higher principles of care. Margaret Thatcher's Conservative governments in the 1980s went further and challenged the post-war political consensus on everything from welfare to employment policy. In the late 1980s the government introduced plans for 'internal markets' in the NHS, where hospitals and GPs would manage their own allocated budgets and contract in medical and other services.

In the 1980s and early 90s the key issue engaged with by most UK medical dramas was the pernicious impact of welfare cuts on the NHS. Anne Karpf has noted the increasing news visibility of 'NHS cuts' and the hospital 'waiting list' (the time patients had to wait for medical treatment).[62] Andy Medhurst argues that the end of *Casualty*'s 1993–4 season 'saw Charlie [the nurse manager and central character] standing in the smoking ruins of Holby General, an image easily read as symbolising the collapse of the post-war welfare state consensus'.[63] As we have seen, medical dramas of the 1980s such as *The Nation's Health* and *Casualty* had an explicit campaigning agenda against the government changes to the NHS and as such they promoted their claims to realism in terms of contemporary relevance.

What was clearly offensive to many on the political Left in the UK was the import of the language and culture of business into healthcare services, particularly the notion of the 'internal market'. Despite this, by the latter half of the 1990s, there was little dissent to the substance of the changes. When the former chairman of the Conservative Party, Cecil Parkinson, argued that 'The introduction of the market into the health service was an essential part of solving its problems' he was endorsing the New Labour government's pledge to 'rule out nothing' (including charges for patients) in its proposed review of the NHS.[64] Nevertheless, the romantic view of the NHS continued to have a strong resonance in the late 1990s when, on the fiftieth anniversary of the NHS the British tabloid *The Mirror* described the NHS as 'a gift to the nation ... 50 years of care' at the same time that the Prime Minister, Tony Blair, 'promised an end to mixed sex wards, patients being abandoned in corridors, bad food, cancelled operations and pompous treatment by high-handed doctors'.

Blair's attack on doctors had been anticipated nearly two decades before on television. In addition to the theme of welfare cuts some medical dramas in the early 1980s began questioning the aloof and impersonal *culture* of doctors. As Anne Karpf notes, G. F. Newman's *The Nation's Health* was a watershed in medical television because it dramatised the iniquitous impact of a male-dominated medical culture:

> Newman delivered an almost unqualified attack on the medical profession. Doctors, under his gaze, emerged as insensitive self-seekers, pondering their next sinecure over the first incision. They blithely offered their services privately in lieu of a lengthy NHS wait. They conspired with drug companies. And they were racist and sexist to a man … The power and aloofness of intimidating consultants and surgeons were depicted with devastating authenticity.[65]

The Nation's Health depicted (usually male) doctors that treat their patients as vehicles for disease and injury rather than individuals, and it introduced some of the key discursive contexts for the medical drama that was to follow: financial shortages, people in desperate need of hospital beds, the erosion of basic services, and patients who were a 'burden on our resources'. *The Nation's Health* was broadcast on what was then seen as the 'alternative' Channel Four, but *Casualty* brought the same issues into the mainstream three years later. By the late 1980s British television and film had produced a number of narratives where doctors and nurses were depicted as flawed and oppressive figures. *The Houseman's Tale* (BBC, 1987) dramatised healthcare professionals as indifferent and often hungover, while *The Singing Detective* (Amiel/BBC, 1986) and *Paper Mask* (Morahan, 1990) depict the health service as corrupt and oppressive. Again, to use Tony Blair's words, it was 'pompous treatment by high-handed doctors' that was the focus of criticism. In *The Singing Detective* the entrance of the senior consultant and his entourage of fawning juniors is accompanied on the soundtrack by G. F. Handel's 'Arrival of the Queen of Sheba'. He gives a patronising diagnosis to the bedridden central character, Philip Marlow (Michael Gambon), who complains to them,

> I don't understand because I seem to have regressed into the helpless and pathetic condition of total dependency. Of the kind normally associated with infancy … The last time I experienced anything remotely like this was in my bloody pram! Being drooled over by slobbering cretins – who turned out to be escapees from the local looney bin. They thought they were doctors and nurses.

Paper Mask has doctors celebrating the acquittal of a colleague, Matthew (Paul McGann), who was accused of killing a patient – in fact Matthew is uneducated and untrained and has been posing as a doctor. His sheer ignorance is greeted with understanding, with one doctor laughing as he says, 'We've all killed a few in our time.' The fact that Matthew fits in at all is part of the film's critique of the dangerous smugness of the closed society of the medical profession.

Outside of film and television the critique of medical culture had been part of a collection of sociological and medical literature written since the late 1960s that had been calling the medical profession into question for the alleged harm it did to its patients. Well-known examples include the work of radical psychiatrists R. D. Laing (whose book *The Divided Self* was the basis of a television play written by David Mercer in 1967, *In Two Minds*) and David Cooper, and sociologist Ivan Illitch. This work that had been largely confined to the fringes was now being mainstreamed in policy and fictional drama during the 1990s. It is worth remembering that in the 1950s television medical dramas and documentaries such as *Your Life in their Hands* (1958) were concerned *not* to encourage anxiety and hypochondria, and to *reassure* the public and the potential patient; they avoided any overt political engagement with the issues of the NHS or critique of the medical profession. Later shows, drawing on the intellectual traditions and cultural penetration of Laing's and Illitch's ideas, aimed to disturb and create popular distrust of the medical profession. This was evident in Hollywood movies as far back as the early 1970s with films such as *The Hospital* (Hiller, 1971) and *Such Good Friends* (Preminger, 1971). The collapse of the post-war consensus and the Soviet Union during the late 1980s contributed to a heightened sense of uncertainty and anxiety that was articulated in popular fiction. Despite the fact that the rapid expansion of healthcare and significant developments in medical science had improved the lives of most people living in the West, there was a growing assumption that medical and social problems could no longer be solved by a value-free science; indeed the claims and ambitions of science and technology were largely viewed with suspicion by the 1990s. It is clear that a post-war optimism in science, medicine and progress had been transformed into a widespread cynicism and suspicion of the medical industry, from drug companies to surgeons to the 'insensitive' local GP.

On both sides of the Atlantic the acknowledgment that healthcare providers had finite, limited resources formed part of the public consciousness, and was a rich source of dramatic narratives. It is relatively easy to see shows such as *Casualty* in the 1980s working through dramas informed by the rhetoric of 'cuts' and various crises of under-funding. Nonetheless the generic structure of the shows revealed a contradiction: the medical staff suffered the pressure but it came from both the government and the patients: doctors themselves would have to make 'tough decisions' regarding the allocation of healthcare services, and 'rationing' became part of the moral framework established in recognition of limited funds. Again, hospital dramas incorporated these inherently dramatic moral dilemmas: should we allocate money to treat the lifetime cigarette smoker or give a child a kidney machine?

In an episode of *Casualty*, 'Hit and Run', we see this kind of news-led campaigning taking place.[66] Over the preceeding two years, there were frequent news stories about the 'winter crisis in the NHS' and such stories had become a generic feature of late summer news in the UK.[67] The fact that some critically ill patients were being transported to far-away hospitals was widely seen as a product of the 'internal market', with hospital trusts soliciting GP fund-holder's budgets. The episode begins with the monotonous sound of the EKG 'flat line' and a close-up of what turns out to be a dead patient. Barbara 'Baz' Samuels (Julia Watson) complains that they have been wasting their time because the man had died in the ambulance during a fifty-mile journey to get to the hospital. A few minutes later Baz breaks the news to the man's wife who wonders, 'Why here? Why fifty miles away?'; 'It's the GP's fault,' replies Baz. It transpires that the wife is considering suing the hospital and in a later conversation with the senior doctor, Mike Barrett (Clive Mantle), Baz explicitly cites the internal market as responsible for the man's death.

This is a good example of the way in which *Casualty* wears its topicality on its sleeve: like other hospitals in the UK, we have a problem with transported patients who require immediate care. *Casualty* illustrates and dramatises the issue – it shows us the product of the policy. It points the finger of blame and uses the grief of the man's wife as a lever to make a political point. The problem with this is that topicality and political sloganeering is presented at the expense of dramatic force. All the scene has going for it is the buzz of the 'contemporary': yes, we might say, I read/heard about this happening for real. *Casualty*'s Holby City is supposed to be Everyhospital. Instead of taking this issue and developing it (in relation to Baz's character), it is left to stand alone. Later scenes with Baz concern her adulterous relationship with Charlie Fairhead, the chief nurse. No further reference is made to the issue or the event. The story feels underlined, served up for us and undeveloped; the inherent drama in a man dying and his wife's grief is served up for the purpose of making what is quite an obvious point about the absurdity of delaying medical treatment. There are no other meanings available when the material is presented in this way – the stand-and-deliver performances of the actors robs them, and the topic, of its dramatic force; the wife and the doctor are in agreement, and we have to be too. Meaning is not made available to be discovered in the interrelationship between event and viewpoint. The responsibility for the meaning is held entirely within the presentation: we are shown how to feel.

Indeed this is a common criticism of medical dramas – the very flexibility and dramatic opportunities offered by the setting – the fact that anyone can walk in, also risks charges of dramatic opportunism. In *Casualty* often what walks in are not patients but 'issues' that the medical staff have to resolve; the injury or illness provides a thin pretext for what is an exploration of a contemporary problem: domestic abuse, homosexuality, the inability to open up and talk out problems. By the late 1990s, however, hospital dramas deliberately avoided 'shortage' narratives where they could. For example, ITV's *Always and Everyone* tends to avoid explicit campaigning: 'Its approach is very unlike *Casualty*'s. It's focused tightly on the hospital setting, concerned chiefly with the core team of staff and in terms of "look", it's more glossy. This is not about the NHS in crisis.'[68]

While the US healthcare context is different it also had to face the various critiques of medical science and practice from the 1970s onwards. There was a critique of medical macho culture and a growing suspicion of medical science's claims of progress towards a healthier (and therefore better) society. There were resonances of such critiques in *M*A*S*H* and *St Elsewhere*. US healthcare provision relies on medical insurance, Medicare and Medicaid plans set up in 1965 to assist the elderly and the poor. Nevertheless it is estimated that in 2000 40 million US citizens did not have medical insurance at all.[69] Consequently many of the potent contemporary issues in new hospital dramas tended to focus on the consequences of patients not having or losing their insurance, and the tough decisions that the medical staff had to make when faced with a patient on limited coverage. The new hospital dramas emerged in the 1990s in the US at a time when healthcare reform was high on the agenda. As the costs of medical insurance skyrocketed HMOs became central in the dispersal and structuring of healthcare provision. The managed care plans that HMOs offered came in for much criticism, particularly in *ER*, since it was alleged that many of them did not provide adequate coverage. For example, in *ER* Kerry Weaver is convinced by Dr Ellis West to allow his company (Synergix Physicians Group Management Consultancy) to manage the care in the ER. Weaver eventually is romantically involved with West which is further complicated when she discovers the company has shut down over half of the ERs it has managed. 'I'm willing to make hard choices [but not] to endanger patients,' Weaver tells Ellis.[70]

Whatever the social specificity of these contexts the debates are dramatised in both the UK and US dramas around the financial limitations of healthcare provision and blame is directed accordingly (at NHS bureaucrats, HMO small print, etc. and the various personifications of these organisations), which is contrasted to the visualisation of the pain and suffering of the patient who cannot afford to pay.

The critique of macho surgeons and GPs developed alongside a different response to the rationing of healthcare (and one that was keenly promoted by HMOs). This was the promotion of health as a strategy for lowering the burden of state and private healthcare provision. During the 1980s and 90s health promotion became a regular feature of everyday life in the West. The media ran detailed campaigns to raise awareness of correct dietary and exercise requirements, alongside the already established (but intensified) anti-smoking and drinking ones. The active promotion of 'healthy living' developed in tandem with the astonishing proliferation of health scares, and both were part of the wider dynamic of the medicalisation of the self.

The medicalised self

Eat, drink, and be merry, for tomorrow we die, has always carried with it the assumption that all three activities directly contribute to the undesired outcome.[71]

That's the trouble with you people – every time you see a problem you turn it into a disease.[72]

That modern societies in the West are experiencing a period of profound identity crisis is by now a cliché. Numerous commentators and scholars have explored the consequences for the western imagination of the end of the Cold War, the erosion of adult solidarity, the popular disengagement with political activity, and the fragmentation of family life.[73] In an atomised and fragmented society the fear of risk-taking, anxiety about our roles in society, and a sense that change is inherently dangerous regularly shape our responses to the world.

The medicalisation of everyday life and the interest in the body as a site of protest and self-expression are important factors in the rise of particular thematic developments in hospital dramas. During the 1990s the body became the privileged site where anxieties, hopes and fear were projected: in social terms the available sphere of action and intervention in the public sphere become radically contracted to the limits of the human body itself. As Tony Soprano's comment suggests, the tendency to perceive any 'unusual' behaviour as pathological is now widespread. Social 'problems' become pathologised so that being fat or thin, or boisterous or shy are now medical conditions – eating disorders, hyperactivity, social phobia.[74] The expansion of lifestyle drugs to treat these problems – Xenical (obesity), Seroxat (shyness) – accompanied by disease awareness campaigns and the promotion of 'healthier lifestyles' has meant an increased visibility of medical care in everyday life. Medical discourses are frequently deployed as an explanatory framework for human behaviour.

Part of this process is the consistent encouragement by state, the medical profession and other 'health awareness' groups for the population to internalise the discourses of medical risk, so that individual decisions once wholly in the sphere of personal taste frequently have to take into account the medical cost to the body. Banal decisions such as, shall I – have another drink? – work late? – have the steak or the fish? become weighted down with the implications of that activity for the health of one's body. Since the relationship between citizen and state is increasingly reified through health promotion, 'taking care of yourself' begins to feel like an oppressive moral duty rather than something freely chosen. It is not so much that people have become hypochondriacs, scouring each television medical drama for confirmation of their pathology, but that the condition of hypochondria has been universalised to the extent that the absence of sensitivity about one's health could be taken as a sign of illness in itself, perhaps aligned with a masculine unwillingness ('maladaptive masculinity') to talk about one's health or sickness, or to make a visit to the doctor.

Most health campaigns attempt to foster feelings of guilt and anxiety and typically deploy a moralising rhetoric. As Michael Fitzpatrick argues, the

> evils targeted by modern health promotion are strikingly similar to the sins defined by traditional religion – from promiscuity to drunkenness and gluttony. In fact today's health moralism is even worse: at least religion accepts the reality of suffering and offers consolation in an afterlife. 'Healthism' offers only fear and guilt.[75]

Accident prevention, the delineation of various toxic interpersonal relationships (between people, parents and children, etc.) forced a sense of risk that meant not only risk to the immediate body but to the psyche imagined as vulnerable as the body itself to the shocks of the world.

The proliferation of health scares reinforced this extension of the medical canopy: from the impact of state-sponsored AIDS-awareness campaigns in the 1980s (linking medicine, morality, sex and disease), to the contraceptive pill and thrombosis, BSE and beef, genetically modified foods, exposure to sunlight and cancer, vaccinations and side-effects, tampons and toxic shock syndrome, nuts and allergies, the emergence of new plagues (Ebola) and the return of old ones (tuberculosis). Most of these scares were speculative and unsubstantiated by reliable scientific evidence, often figuring as vague 'syndromes' with associative, rather than causal, links. The command model for the contemporary health scare was the AIDS panic of the 1980s, where the emergence of a new disease provided the opportunity for the state and medical profession to intervene in the lifestyle of citizens using a powerful moralising discourse. Despite the fact that those at most risk were homosexual men the disease was framed as a threat to everyone, seriously misrepresenting the risk to heterosexuals. The panic used medical discourses as a means of intervening in the most intimate aspects of individual lives, no doubt creating much unnecessary anxiety.[76] An important aspect of the scare was the possibility that doctors and surgeons could acquire and transmit the disease during their treatment of patients, a powerful theme that is frequently developed by medical dramas.

Such panics, scares and methods of health promotion actually contribute to a world where illness is no longer the 'deviant' state it was once perceived to be.[77] What is striking, in the fictional and real world, is the transition from seeing illness as deviance from the healthy norm, to illness as a norm itself. In his book, *Culture of Fear*, sociologist Frank Furedi notes that there has been a 66 per cent rise in self-reported long-term illnesses in Britain since 1972, and that between 1985 and 1996 the number of people who considered themselves disabled increased by 40 per cent. This is paradoxically dependent on the fact of vastly improved standards of health in the West:

> we are confronted with the paradox that the healthier we are, the more likely we are to define ourselves as ill ... this sense of the diseased self expresses profound anxieties about a world that seems so threatening. In such circumstances, illness becomes the norm – to be alive is to be ill.[78]

Furedi's argument rests on his assertion that people are generally more isolated, atomised and that the breakdown of adult solidarity – traditional family and kinship ties and collective organisations – results in a loneliness and insecurity that breeds fear and anxiety, and, ultimately, a loss of confidence in the ability of the human subject to transcend these problems.[79]

The interest in illness, death and the body was also widespread in artistic, journalistic and academic work.[80] For example, in the mid-1990s extracts from the novelist Harold Brodkey's journal, which he kept while dying from AIDS, were published in a national newspaper.[81] Roy Greenslade, defending the mode of journalism that Mick Hume has described as the 'celebrity cancer column' (writings by sick or dying journalists such as Ruth Picardie, Oscar Moore, John Diamond), argues that 'Many of us "healthy" readers now understand more about cancer, its treatment and its effects, physical and psychological because of [John Diamond]'.[82] The conditional quotes around healthy signify the widespread belief that none of us are, at heart, really well. As James Halloran argues in the US context:

> The important point is ... not that everyone is sick or that everyone understands himself or herself to be sick. ... What is important to recognise is that it is increasingly acceptable, on a cultural level, to understand oneself and to speak of oneself according to these [pathological] categories. ... the sickness, disease, and addiction concepts serve as increasingly acceptable symbolic reference points.[83]

The prevalence of the morbid and ghoulish imagination in many societies during the 1990s was no doubt connected to a sense of the body and its decay as a locus of experiencing the self. It is a fascination that signals the collapse of imagination onto the body itself. In 2001 there was a sensational scandal in the UK concerning organs removed from dead children during autopsies without the consent of their parents; this was reported in ghoulish detail by the media. In terms of fine art the fascination with the traumatised body was rapidly becoming a cliché by the late 1990s. The body and its effluent became a medium of art: Tracey Emin's work perhaps best exemplifies this fascination with the degraded human body. As Joanna Briscoe notes,

> Body obsession has reached epidemic proportions. The body is mutable, no longer a given configuration of flesh, features and genes, but the chosen canvas of the decade, the clay of a booming industry, its internal workings forming the bloody landscape of a wilderness.[84]

In October 2000 the Hayward Gallery in London launched an exhibition, 'Spectacular Bodies: the Art and Science of the Human Body from Leonardo to Now', bringing a range of exhibits from medical and art galleries across the world, such as a preserved eighteenth-century foetus adorned with beads. Many anti-abortion and Christian groups objected to the exhibition but the Hayward's curator, Margot Heller, argued that the wider public already had a taste for it, 'The idea of squeamishness and trying to define that is fascinating. There are people who faint at the sight of blood and others who are totally addicted to *ER* and *Casualty*.'[85] Hospital dramas themselves acknowledged and ridiculed such art: in an episode of *ER* an artist with a gunshot wound to the leg refuses painkillers – 'let my body be the canvas, I want to experience the pain' – to the bemusement and derision of the medical staff.[86]

To some extent *ER* offers a corrective to the articulations of medicine and medical care one finds in academic work on the body.[87] Much of that scholarship makes claims about the transgressive potential of the body or its obsolescence; in contrast *ER* and other new hospital dramas visualise the persistence of the body as a source of narrative drama. They figure it as a dramatic *device*. By articulating, working through and imagining the drama of the body and its narratives of pain and suffering they allow it to become a true dramatic canvas. Also, they humanise the bodies of their patients, so that they are always attributed a name, a subjectivity, a history, a humanity – many of the qualities that some scholarship would posit as obsolete in themselves.

Even fictional characters are vulnerable to medical explanation. What in the past were considered complex characters are now discussed in the language of medical pathology. Talking about the depiction of Miss Haversham in the BBC's adaptation of *Great Expectations* (1999), the producer David Snodin remarked, 'she's a quintessential clinical depressive. She's an agoraphobic who won't wash. These days she'd be on Prozac – and it wouldn't do her any good.'[88] The fact that Snodin used the language of medicine in order to paint a cogent picture for a popular audience is indicative of the penetration of medical terminology in everyday life. To a certain extent the internalisation of the medical discourse means that we have all become amateur pharmacists, psychologists and GPs, placing our bodies and minds under anxious self-surveillance.

Given this rather gloomy account of some of the discursive contexts of contemporary healthcare it may seem rather paradoxical that the new hospital dramas are often perceived as 'sexy and post-modern'. In a nod to the extension of medical discourse, the cover of the BBC listings magazine, the *Radio Times*, promised to explain 'Why we're addicted to medical dramas', providing a strong visual hint with its image of *Chicago Hope*'s Mandy Patinkin and *Cardiac Arrest*'s Helen Baxendale. But it is not the juxtaposition of glamour and morbidity alone that encourages us to watch. While there is no doubt that medical dramas offer the promise of glamour in terms of star appeal, this hardly begins to explain the potential seduction of the visualisation of medical procedures, illness and death.

My argument is that medical dramas examine the contemporary self-in-the-world and the world-in-the-self, a self that is perceived as vulnerable, sick or dying. In this way I am arguing contrary to A. A. Gill's suggestion that medical dramas 'entice you to identify with the fit and the strong and to despise the halt and the weak' and claiming that they ask us to acknowledge our own vulnerability and mortality especially in their depictions of body trauma.[89]

Notes

1. A very early example of this is the US single play 'The Hospital' where a disturbed porter disrupts the power supply to the hospital. It was a CBS/*Studio One* production broadcast 10–11pm, Monday 8 December 1952. It was directed by Franklin Schaffner.
2. *Playing Doctor* (BBC, 1996); Alan Alda responds, 'Imitation is the sincerest form of television – they copy everything.'
3. *M*A*S*H* was based on the 1970 film of the same name; the director, Robert Altman, complained that 'The series was done for commerce, not for art.' Joseph Turow, *Playing*

Doctor: Television, Storytelling and Medical Power (Oxford: Oxford University Press, 1989), p. 212.

4. For UK broadcasts the laugh track was deleted to admirable effect so that it was possible to respond freely to what was happening instead of being guided by laugh-track cues. This made it far less clear whether some lines were intended for comedy or not which reinforced the show's edgy irony.

5. Turow, *Playing Doctor*, p. 206.

6. Ibid., p. 212.

7. David Marc cites Larry Gelbart's claim that '... many of the episodes that centred on the doctor's troubles were metaphorically drawn from our own conflicts with the CBS brass'. *Comic Visions: Television Comedy and American Culture*, second edition (Malden: Blackwell, 1997), p. 159.

8. Alan Alda speaking in *Playing Doctor* (BBC, 1996).

9. This is Larry Gelbart, in Turow, *Playing Doctor*, p. 197. As Turow notes there had been other medical sitcoms in the 1960s: *Hennesey*, *Julia* and *Temperatures Rising*. *M*A*S*H* premiered in September 1972 and ended in 1983.

10. Ibid., p. 207.

11. Andrew Calcutt, *Arrested Development: Pop Culture and the Erosion of Adulthood* (London: Cassell, 1998), p. 168.

12. Turow, *Playing Doctor*, p. 214.

13. John Caldwell, *Televisuality: Style, Crisis and Authority in American Television* (New Brunswick, NJ: Rutgers University Press, 1995), p. 61.

14. Marc, *Comic Visions*, p. 159.

15. Calcutt, *Arrested Development*, pp. 127–9.

16. Stanley Cavell, 'The Fact of Television' in *Themes Out of School: Effects and Causes* (Chicago, IL: University of Chicago Press, 1984), pp. 235–68.

17. V. F. Perkins, *Film as Film* (Harmondsworth: Pelican, 1972), p. 151.

18. Quoted in Turow, *Playing Doctor*, p. 239. Turow notes the influence of Asher Shem's novel, *The House of God*, which is a cynical view of a teaching hospital. It has the populist existential despair rendered in a comic manner.

19. Turow, *Playing Doctor*, p. 247.

20. Ibid., p. 268.

21. Hilary Kingsley, *Casualty: The Inside Story* (London: BBC Books, 1993).

22. Quoted in ibid., p. 7.

23. Brock and Unwin interviewed on *Playing Doctor* (BBC, 1996).

24. Kingsley, *Casualty*, p. 8.

25. Ibid., p. 17.

26. Quoted in Meg Carter, 'Carry on, matron', *The Guardian* (15 September 2000).

27. A former writer for the show told me that writing it was like 'filling out a crossword puzzle'.

28. Spielberg's Amblin Television and Crichton's Constant C Productions co-produce the show with Warners Television for the NBC network.

29. Warner Bros *ER* website: <www2.warnerbros.com/ertv/home.html>.

30. Quoted in Jane Cassidy and Diane Taylor, 'Doctor, doctor, where can I get an aspirin', *The Guardian* (12 December 1997).

31. *The Larry Sanders Show*, 'Eight', season 4, episode 16 (1995).

32. Warner Bros *ER* website: <www2.warnerbros.com/ertv/home.html>.

33. Cassidy and Taylor, 'Doctor, doctor, where can I get an aspirin'.

34. 'Docs on the Box', 9 June 1996, BBC2. For full details see *Radio Times* (8–14 June 1996), p. 70. 'Cops on the Box', 31 May 1993, BBC2. For programme details see *Radio Times* (29 May–4 June 1993), p. 74. Channel Four offered a theme weekend in 1995 on television's uber-genre, 'Soap Opera Weekend'.

35. Charlotte Brunsdon, 'Structure of anxiety: recent British television crime fiction', *Screen*, vol. 39, no. 3 (Autumn 1998), p. 32.

36. *Playing Doctor* (BBC, 1996).

37. Karen Lury, 'Television Performance: Being, Acting and "Corpsing"', *New Formations*, no. 26 (1995–6); Brunsdon, 'Structure of anxiety.'

38. Steve Bailey, '"Professional Television": Three (Super) Texts and a (Super) Genre', *The Velvet Light Trap*, no. 47 (Spring 2001), p. 55.

39. Television Studies itself became prominent as a discipline in the 1980s.

40. Andy Medhurst, 'Still hooked on pulse fiction', *The Sunday Times* (30 April 1995), p. 13. Virginia Bottomley was UK Secretary of State for Health 1992–5.

41. See Deborah Thomas, *Beyond Genre: Melodrama, Comedy and Romance in Hollywood Films* (Moffat: Cameron Books, 2000).

42. Michael Fitzpatrick, *The Tyranny of Health: Doctors and the Regulation of Lifestyle* (London: Routledge, 2001), p. 158.

43. John Ellis, *Seeing Things: Television in the Age of Uncertainty* (London: I. B. Tauris, 2000), pp. 78–9.

44. The scholarships I am thinking of that seem to offer ways into addressing this question are, Siegfried Kracauer, *From Caligari to Hitler* (Princeton, NJ: Princeton University Press, 1974); Richard Dyer, 'Entertainment and Utopia', *Movie*, no. 24 (Spring 1977) and Raymond Williams, *Television: Technology and Cultural Form* (London: Fontana, 1974).

45. Thomas Schatz, 'Workplace Programs', in Horace Newcomb (ed.), *The Encyclopedia of Television*, vol. 3 (Chicago, IL: Fitzroy Dearborn, 1997), p. 1873.

46. Bailey, '"Professional Television"', p. 46.

47. Steven Poole, 'Whoa! I gotta pumper!', *Times Literary Supplement* (2 February 1996), p. 18.

48. Ibid. See also Jason Jacobs, 'Gunfire', in Karl French (ed.), *Screen Violence* (London: Bloomsbury, 1996), for an account of how action films dramatise the loss of responsibility for the body.

49. For an attempt to theorise the flexibility of modern television narratives see Robin Nelson, *TV Drama in Transition: Forms, Values and Cultural Change* (Houndmills: Macmillan, 1997).

50. Turow, *Playing Doctor*, p. 75.

51. Robert J. Elisberg, 'E-mail interview with Carol Flint', <www.wga.org/craft/interviews/flint.html> (link expired, 11 February 2003).

52. *ER*, 'Blizzard', season 1, episode 9 (1994).

53. His death and its impact on his colleagues and family is dramatised in 'The Letter' and 'On the Beach', *ER* season 8, episodes 20 and 21 (2002).

54. Greene is the natural successor to the major television doctor/humanists that came before him, James Kildare and Benjamin 'Hawkeye' Pierce, although they never had to suffer to the extent he does.

55. Russell Jacoby, *The End of Utopia: Politics and Culture in an Age of Apathy* (New York, NY: Basic Books, 1999), p. 155.

56. John O'Reilly, 'The real macabre', *The Guardian* (3 July 1995) p. 4.

57. Ibid.

58. Poole, 'Whoa! I gotta pumper!' p. 18.

59. Mark Lawson, 'Over here and doing fine', *New Statesman and Society* (24 May 1996), p. 17.

60. Jim Shelley, 'Fatal attractions', *The Sunday Times* (13 September 1992). '[*Casualty* is] a hard, fast, exhilarating assault, a catalogue of modern horrors ...', p. 8.

61. Brunsdon, 'Structure of anxiety: recent British television crime fiction'.

62. See Anne Karpf, *Doctoring the Media* (London: Routledge, 1988), pp. 30–1. The rhetoric of cuts has an impact elsewhere, not least in the institutions of television itself. During the late 1980s and 90s, the BBC continued to cut its staff. Director General John Birt announced a further 20 per cent cutback in programme budgets and more job losses 'to fund the digital revolution'. 'In the past three years the BBC has cut 4000 jobs from a workforce of 22000 in its drive for efficiency.' *The Times* (9 July 1997).

63. Medhurst, 'Still hooked on pulse fiction'.

64. *Any Questions*, BBC Radio 4 (14 June 1997).

65. Karpf, *Doctoring the Media*, p. 199.

66. *Casualty*, 'Hit and Run', season 10, episode 9 (1995).

67. In July 1997, doctors announced that hospitals would only be able to handle emergencies during the winter and it was alleged that seriously ill patients were 'roaming the country' looking for beds. According to a spokesman, Dr Macara, 'We cannot continue to be forced to work in a system in which the pressures are those of a business-driven enterprise while the rewards are those of a care-driven service.' *The Times* (1 July 1997).

68. Pamela Wilson, producer, quoted in Carter, 'Carry on, matron'.

69. Lynne Page Snyder, 'The Uninsured: Myths and Realities', *Issues in Science and Technology Online* (Winter 2001).

70. See *ER*, season 4, episodes 6–13 (1998).

71. Anthony J. Cleare and Simon C. Wessely, 'Just what the doctor ordered – more alcohol and sex', *British Medical Journal*, no. 315 (20 December 1997), pp. 1637–8.

72. Tony Soprano (James Gandolfini), *The Sopranos*, 'Down Neck' (HBO, 1999); thanks to Michael Fitzpatrick for finding this in his article, 'ADHD: Turning a Problem Into a Disease', *Spiked*, 29 December 2000, <www.spiked-online.com>.

73. The best known are Anthony Giddens, *Modernity and Self Identity: Self and Society in the Late Modern Age* (Cambridge: Polity Press, 1991); *Runaway World: How Globalisation is Reshaping Our Lives* (London: Profile Books, 1999); Ulrich Beck, *Risk Society: Towards a New Modernity* (London: Sage, 1992) and *The Brave New World of Work* (Cambridge: Polity Press, 2000); and Francis Fukuyama, *The Great Disruption: Human Nature and the Reconstitution of Social Order* (New York, NY: Free Press, 1999) and *Our Posthuman Future* (London: Profile Books, 2000).

74. A recent example of this trend is the discovery of NES – night eating syndrome (raiding the fridge at night for snacks) – a combination of an eating disorder, a sleeping disorder and a mood disorder. See also Elaine Showalter, *Hystories: Hysterical Epidemics and Modern Media* (New York, NY: Columbia University Press, 1997).

75. Michael Fitzpatrick, 'Healthy eating in a diseased society', *LM* no. 75 (January 1995), p. 22.

76. See Simon Watney, 'The political significance of statistics in the AIDS crisis: epidemiology, representation and re-gaying', in Joshua Oppenheimer and Helena Reckitt (eds), *Acting on AIDS, sex, drugs and politics* (London: Serpent's Tail, 1997) and Fitzpatrick, *Tyranny of Health*, pp. 14–15.

77. See Joan Liebmann-Smith and Sharon L. Rosen, 'The Presentation of Illness on Television', in Charles Winick, *Deviance and the Mass Media* (London: Sage, 1978), pp. 79–80.

78. Frank Furedi, 'Feeding off the culture of fear', *LM*, no. 119 (April 1999), p. 31.

79. See Frank Furedi, *Culture of Fear: Risk-Taking and the Morality of Low Expectation* (London: Cassell, 1997); Furedi expands this argument in his book, *Paranoid Parenting* (London: Allen Lane, 2001).

80. For example, see Bryan S. Turner, *The Body and Society*, second edition (London: Sage, 1996); Lisa Cartwright, 'Community and the public body in breast cancer media activism', *Cultural Studies*, vol. 12, no. 2 (1998), pp. 117–38, which attempts to understand the paradox of postmodernism's celebration of difference and fragmentation with the desire for community and identity. Florence Jacobowitz and Richard Lippe, 'Todd Haynes' *Safe*: Illness as Metaphor in the 90s', celebrate that film whose central figure is a sick vulnerable woman – her sickness caused by pollution, so that the film's 'sombre conclusions can be read as a form of protest'. *CineAction* no. 43 (July 1997).

81. See for example, *The Times* 5 November 1996; Harold Brodkey, *The Wild Darkness: The Story of My Death* (London: Fourth Estate, 1996).

82. Roy Greenslade, *The Guardian* (3 March 1999). John Diamond was a columnist for *The Times* who wrote about his own throat cancer.

83. James Halloran, *The Therapeutic State* (New York, NY: New York University Press, 1998), p. 14.

84. Joanna Briscoe, 'The skull beneath the skin', *The Guardian* (18 February 1997).

85. Reported in *The Times* (15 September 2000).

86. *ER*, 'Ground Zero', season 4, episode 6 (1998).

87. For a very full list of scholarly work on the body see, 'Beauty and the Body in Film, Television, and Popular Culture: A Bibliography', *The Velvet Light Trap*, no. 49 (Spring 2002).

88. James Rampton, 'On the darker side of Dickens', *The Times* (10 April 1998).

89. A. A. Gill, *The Sunday Times* (17 January 1999).

2

The Body in Ruins: Action and Spectacle

Give me a good sick body needs a little slicing, and I'm a happy man.[1]

Whoaa! I got a pumper![2]

The explicit visualisation of emergency treatment was one of the most distinctive features of the new hospital drama. Graphic depictions of serious injury became the norm with bleeding wounds, screaming patients and fast-talking medical staff key elements in the *mise en scène*. Like medical dramas before them, *ER*, *Chicago Hope* and *Cardiac Arrest* promoted their novelty in terms of greater verisimilitude, promising to show the audience what it was really like to work in a busy emergency department. At the same time they were all heavily stylised. Before the 1980s the depiction of injury was relatively restrained and only *Casualty* was willing to regularly showcase the details of body trauma. In order to understand the changes in the genre we need to explore the origins of this realistic and speedy style which derives from the cluster of genres collectively known as 'reality TV'.

Reality TV
Reality TV emerged as a successful, cheap format in the US in the early 1990s and initially adopted the address of factual news magazine programmes. As Jon

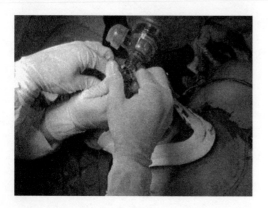

'the aesthetic kick of the visceral':
close-up emergency care in *ER*

Dovey notes these shows were typically based around the activities of the emergency services, 'programmes based on crime, accident and health stories, what we might call "trauma TV"'.[3] A typical example of reality TV in this period combined authentic found footage with witness testimony linked by an omniscient narrative voice. Generally, these shows attempted to combine a moral or public service safety address, with an explicitly tabloid voyeurism.

The rise of reality TV in the US was partly a response to economic pressure in the television industry during the early 1990s, where high-risk drama formats such as *Twin Peaks* and *China Beach* were abandoned in favour of cheaper reality shows. During the 1990–91 programming year inexpensive shows such as *Cops*, *Rescue 911* and *America's Funniest Home Videos* were very popular. They relied on footage originated from camcorders, or on low-tech reconstructions offering a variously stylised platter of low-resolution images.[4] At the end of the industry recession in 1993 there was a resurgence in hour-long prime-time drama programming, with many of the traditional genres absorbing some of the stylistic rhetorics of reality programming as well as acknowledging their voyeuristic impulse. For example, *Homicide: Life on the Street* and *NYPD Blue* integrated a voyeuristic interest in professional life with stylistic ambition and innovation.

In addition, the reality TV formats of the early 1990s consolidated and popularised a number of stylistic and aesthetic strategies that had been developed earlier in documentary film. Importantly they promoted the idea that televisual space was no longer *necessarily* narrativised. The camera could be imaging 'dead' empty space, but that only contributed to the sense of contingent reality in the frame. As a consequence of this, *mise en scène* was less about staging events for the camera than discovering them, and the increased mobility of the televisual frame was expressive of the attempt to catch up with events as they happened. In reality TV, found video footage was edited down to the most dramatic moments and there was a quick alternation of narrative segments so that the rapid turnover of events were set to a speedy editing pace and tempo. It is clear that this pace and tempo were imported directly into the new hospital dramas with *ER* probably the most striking example of a show that owes a debt to non-fiction 'documentary' visual styles. This was not at the expense of character development or narrative complexity or the distinctions sought by quality drama series. Indeed some episodes of *ER* (most obviously *ER*'s live episode 'Ambush') explicitly distanced themselves from the assumed sensationalism and cheapness of some reality television shows.

The development of hospital drama in the 1990s in relation to changes in reality television programming is only part of the picture: as we have seen, the routine generic figuring of the hospital as a war zone evinced by *M*A*S*H* and *Casualty* was refined during this period. Conflict, violence and war were crucial features in the television landscape of the early 1990s such as the rolling news coverage of the Gulf War and the LA riots, and the video footage of the Rodney King beating. In addition the rise in action cinema during the 1990s contributed to the way in which fast-paced, spectacle-hungry moments of emergency treatment were constructed in visual and narrative spaces (for example, *ER* frequently showed slow-motion shootings, explosions, crashes and helicopter flights).[5] It was the frantic action elements of *ER* and *Chicago Hope* that critics responded to.

As we saw in the previous chapter, the mid-1990s critical response to reality TV and new hospital and crime fiction often saw them together as a manifestation of unhealthy audience appetites. John O'Reilly described these 'virulently voyeuristic' modes as part of the desire for more immediate reality: 'we will turn on to anything that just might sate our desire to get up close to real events, raw emotion, and authentic feeling.'[6] The style of the shows was expressive of that uncertain reality and the viewer was anchored to the images from the hand-held camera so that, 'In life or death situations the panic the camera conveys lets us know just how shaky things really are.'[7] Jim Shelley argued that the shows were a product of modern life:

> *Casualty* is a sign of the times, our television times and otherwise, the hospital drama version of *Driller Killer*. From the opening credits and theme music onward, it is a hard, fast, exhilarating assault, a catalogue of modern horrors that has condemned predecessors such as *Dr Kildare*, *Ben Casey*, *Emergency Ward 10*, *St Elsewhere* to the status of historical relics.[8]

For Shelley the popular attraction of
lay in its no-holds-barred attention to graphic visceral detail:

> Expectations were rightly high for the start of the new 24–episode series, particularly as the corresponding episode last year featured the daring helicopter rescue of a teenage rock-climber whose leg had been graphically mangled by a rock fall and needed to be amputated (in gory close-up) before gangrene set in.[9]

The 'unhealthy' visual appetites of the viewing population seemed to be confirmed in the UK in August 1996 when footage of operations was released on the video *Everyday Operations*. It showed mainly brain and eye operations and was promptly banned by the government, but its mere existence seemed to confirm both the unlikely idea that surgeons needed to make money on the side and that there was a market for it. As *The Times* of London put it, 'There can be little doubt that the video's intended market is those with a ghoulish tendency who enjoy traffic accidents and medical soaps.'[10] To an extent that appetite was identified and extrapolated from the hospital shows' own visual style where the camera and its movement was very often expressive of a voyeuristic appetite. That such appetites are imagined, if not actually real, is confirmed by the scheduling in the late 1990s and early twenty-first century of shows such as *The World's Most Shocking Medical Videos* (Fox, 1999–) which offer explicit uncut footage of operations and a *smorgasbord* of freakish deformities for public consumption.

Camera mobility

Most critics interpreted this new interest in medical body horror as indicative of a wider sense of fragility and uncertainty in the world, something expressed stylistically in reality shows and new hospital dramas. Increased camera mobility emerged as a stylistic feature of television in the 1980s, augmented by the adoption of video-assist that removed the camera viewfinder from the camera operator's eyes, and the gradual adoption of elaborate and flexible camera mountings permitted stylistic exhibitionism that 'allow[ed] television cinematographers to shift from sweeping renditions of exterior action to snaking arterial moves through microscopic spaces as well'.[11] As John Caldwell argues: 'This family of motion-control devices all do one thing for the television image: they automate an inherently omniscient point of view and subjectivise it around a technological rather than a human center.'[12] He goes on to note that these styles were promoted in terms of athletics as well as aesthetics so that 'media practitioners now explicitly describe their art in physical, active, and bodily terms'. Hence we get a camera style derived from a mounting that is inherently embodied and yet reduces any sign of the body. A mobile camera style is the genre-innovative aspect of hospital drama 'action' scenes that is most readily appreciable. The first episode of *ER* (excluding the pilot) begins with the case of a baby who is brought in because he has stopped breathing. Dr Susan Lewis (Sherry Stringfield) is called to attend, with four nurses assisting, and the two parents looking on, horrified by the prospect of their child's death. The camera circles the treatment bed and as it does so the image achieves an evolving variation in what it shows. No one is favoured in this shot, but it has the effect of showing a group activity in action with the circling movement underlining a feeling of tense urgency. It is also an efficient way to reveal an economy of looks between the medical staff and between the parents – looks that are variously concerned, diagnostic, compassionate or anxious.

Continuous camera mobility in the long take is one choice. During this sequence we return to a simple process of decoupage: shots of the worried parents; a close shot of Susan looking into the throat of the child; and a broader shot of Susan to contextualise that look in relation to what she is doing with her hands (using tweezers to remove the blockage from the baby's airway).

ER and other new hospital dramas take advantage of emergency treatment to justify an appropriately speedy and 'urgent' style that presents such treatment in a vigorous and dynamic manner. Since the urgency arises from the dramatic situation, this seems less like flaunting the mobile virtuosity of the camera for its own sake, and more like taking advantage of camera mobility in order to direct emphasis to what is already a dramatic situation. Nonetheless, the mobility itself gives more energy to a rapidly shifting series of narrative spaces.

UK and US hospital dramas often differ in their approach to action scenes, with *Casualty*, *Cardiac Arrest* and *Always and Everyone* favouring montage, the fast editing of shots to create emphasis and rhythm compared to the US shows' preference for long takes. As V. F. Perkins notes, the advantage of 'conventional analytic editing' is its 'flexibility, its immediacy of response to dramatic developments, its ability to use the impact of visual shock in the instant transformation of the image, and its capacity for eloquence in playing with and against our interests and expectations'.[13]

The long take with a mobile camera can achieve different effects. There is a camera mobility that seems embodied – it reacts to new events, swiftly and with a motion akin to the sudden turn of the head in apprehension of something important and urgent so that the camera seems to mimic the reactions and anticipation of the human body. By contrast, in *ER* the movement of the camera and its responsiveness seems firmly anchored – as if to a crane or crab – and it is a 'knowing camera', clearly rehearsed yet also able to imply spontaneity. It directs attention, and anticipates, but its very careful choreography does not imply the spontaneous reactivity of the vérité or reality TV style. Hence *ER*'s mobile camera holds in tension the contrived – the planned rehearsed chaos of the trauma room – and the spontaneous, the unexpected. It is a delicate balance, because over-choreographed style draws attention to itself at the expense of what it is showing. The opening of Robert Altman's *The Player* (1992) suffers from this sense of the contrived with characters entering the frame just in time to meet the camera's movement. It feels planned, which is what it is, but the movement and performances appear subordinate to the mobile long take, not the other way around. *ER* succeeds where *The Player* fails in not allowing its mobile virtuosity to overcome the dramatic potential inherent in the setting: this is a busy *emergency* room where things have to move quickly. While this does not necessarily demand a fast mobile camera style, it is one that grows naturally from the dramatic action. The overall emphasis on the balance between speed, motion and character development is emphasised in the title sequences of these shows, and each one underscores the importance of speed and action in the new hospital dramas.

Title sequences

The importance of action for the new hospital dramas is part of the promotional address of their title sequences. I want to examine them in some detail in order to show how action receives differential expression in the branding of each show. As Jostein Gripsrud notes,

> the title sequence of a show is its self-presentation and self-promotion. It is made with particular attention to its audible qualities, so that its particular music etc. can signal throughout its viewers' homes that a particular show is about to start. ... Since they are designed to identify a particular show, they will try to capture and express a particular affective mode which the producers wish to associate with it.[14]

Like the covers of books and magazines, title sequences have communicative and expressive functions that reveal the nature, tone and interests of the show. The new hospital dramas emphasised speed, multiple characters and an interest in medical textures. Those dramas that inhabit the traditional genre remain attached to the rendering of narrative information. As I demonstrate below, we can begin to understand the generic differences between old and new medical dramas by looking at the ways in which their title sequences aspire to different effects.

The title sequence of ER (first season) only lasts for around fifty seconds, and is characterised by the fast tempo of the music and the very fast cutting. Throughout the sequence there is a repeated flashing insistence on the letters 'ER', which fulfils the basic requirement of communicating the name of the show. The necessary opacity of the text credits is contrasted with a series of bluey-white semi-transparent layers (which connotes lit X-ray film), which sweep over (although it could be, in various instances, beneath) the text credit and the moving images.

The title of the programme is of course a shortened speedier way of saying 'emergency room'; intermittently we see this process of abbreviation and fragmentation acted out in the sequence with the words 'emergency room' typed in lower case, with some of its letters being highlighted intermittently in bold. This is expressive of, not so much typing, as monitoring; it both 'explains' the meaning of 'er' the abbreviation, and expresses the show's interests in the monitoring of life and death. This lower case text is contrasted with the emphatic capitalisation of 'ER' that is put through a variety of instantiations – black on white lettering in a box-frame, zoomed in and out, superimposed, and subliminally etched on glass against a white background. Most commonly the 'ER box' is propelled back into the screen, so that there is an odd rendering of perspectival depth using what is in fact a flat surface. The appearance of text –

ER's title sequence: abbreviation and
fragmentation

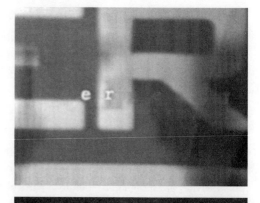

Perspectival depth and flat surfaces

Layered textures

Mobile observation: Mark Greene
(Anthony Edwards)

usually 'hard' and lucid, but here variously lit and mobile – is contrasted with and integrated into the moving images. In fact there are a variety of fonts used: the actors' credits for the show are white, in a font that smooths the edges of its letters; we also see a fragment of writing on the corner of an X-ray film, alongside a photographic calibration scale, and the reflection of the lit sign, 'EMERGENCY ROOM' in a puddle of water (itself contributing to the motif of layering, since the bubbles on its surface partially obscure the reflection of the sign). Another kind of texture – the viscous oozing of red blood – is briefly signalled towards the end of the sequence, in a suitably shocking contrast to the colder blue and white tones of the other textures and surfaces.

The moving image shots that are integrated into this blending of medical textures, fonts and abstract surfaces, appear as fragments of longer shots. As if switching between monitors we get the sense of coverage rather than narrative design: they are expressive of the details of medical procedure. We see a pair of anonymous hands holding up an X-ray film, gloved hands working on a patient, two pairs of running legs, etc. These anonymous fragments are stitched between the shots of the central characters. In the first season there are six main characters: Mark Greene (Anthony Edwards), Doug Ross (George Clooney), Susan Lewis (Sherry Stringfield), John Carter (Noah Wyle), Peter Benton (Eriq LaSalle) and Carol Hathaway (Julianna Margulies) and what we see of them seem to be fragments of longer moments – Benton running through a room into close-up before looking down a corridor, Carter running with the paddles of a defibrillator – and they are used not only to present the main characters but to continue the overall theme that emphasises the urgency of emergency care, something augmented by the cutting into an 'already mobile' shot.

The sound of the title sequence is crucial to the overall effect. *ER*'s title music is usually book-ended with loud, crashing 'impact' sounds before the main theme starts. This begins with fragments of music in a high key, backed by the quiet percussive rhythms of a drum machine. As the volume increases so does the sense of aural space and simultaneously we begin to hear distant electronic echoes, synthesised versions of strings that mimic but also distort (they sound as if in reverse) the sound of ambulance sirens. Indeed many of the sounds we hear are 'variations on a siren theme', a sound that not only connotes ambulance sirens, but also makes them musical (there is clearly a debt to ambient and trance genres of electronic music here). There is a contrast between sounds that are high and low, between layers of sound textures and between the development of a musical theme and the reiteration of percussive interruption – a crashing bass drum beat. This is building to the main theme, which is announced by a much louder bass note, and which then regularly punctuates the next twenty seconds or so until the theme once again builds to an emphatic bass crash. The sequence exploits the effects of the drum machine – allowing the mimicry of cymbal and the high-hat, while using the synthesiser's ability to create a sense of expanding and diminishing sound spaces through its versions of attack and decay, and the swift building of crescendo.

The music is, like the visuals, layered and fragmentary; it naturalistically signals the themes of the show – the arrival of ambulance, the sudden noise of a crash (connoting crashing doors), the sudden unexpected event, the shock of defibrillation – while pushing these connotative sounds through a series of stylisations. It creates an extraordinary sensation of repeated impacts set against a rather mournful – yet fast and bold – main theme.

The sound works with the images but is careful to avoid an insistent mickey-mousing of sound and action; some musical climaxes are anchored to character movement and cutting tempo, but this happens relatively infrequently, and does not distract us by implying a pattern of linkage between the two. (This kind of patterning is something more pronounced in subsequent seasons where the crashing punctuation of the musical theme is anchored to images of doors being banged open, gurney wheels jolting over doorways, Benton punching the air, etc.) Neither does the sequence impose a narrative explanation on what we see: everything signals the urgency of immediate medical care, but the images and sounds do not tell a specific story.

Hence the title sequence is expressive of the style of the show: speedy reactions to medical emergencies, treated by medical staff that are variously concerned, introspective, alone or triumphant. The titles imply the tension between action – the immediate shock of an emergency and its treatment – and reflection – the consequences of that treatment – that the show is so good at imagining. Vigour and boldness in the presentation is matched by subtlety in weaving the various characters within the same stylistic rhetoric, so that the overall flow of the sequence is not compromised by our attention being drawn to one or two characters in particular. Finally, we should note that the sequence's fast-paced style is at the service of the juxtaposition of morbidity and glamour. Indeed one might speculate that this was precisely the problem that its creators had to face: how to badge a show that regularly explored trauma, disease and death in such a way as to make it attractive to audiences.

One moment stands out and is important insofar as it is one of the few retained, in different order of presentation, throughout eight seasons of *ER*. The shot of Mark Greene, seated and gracefully moving backwards on the wheels of his chair, looking off-screen. It immediately tells us about the character's attentiveness and is also expressive of the show's interest in the doctor's (rather than the patient's) reactions to medical emergency. More than that however, it signals the importance of *mobile observation* as both something that the characters have to do in the show *and* the show's stylistic preference, its way of showing what they do. Almost all the shots, as well as the music and the blending of graphical details, are expressive of this stylistic preference. As John Caldwell notes, over 94 per cent of the shots in the first season of *ER* were achieved using the steadicam and the fast mobility of the continuous shot has become a signature style of the show.[15] Greene's movement then is both indicative of his character – cautiously and knowledgably observant and concerned – *and* a reinforcement of the show's stylistic ambitions.

The title sequence follows the brief teaser and the crashing impact of its opening bars is often used to dramatically underline narrative revelations or enigmas. For example, the teaser for 'Long Day's Journey' begins with an action sequence, a young woman with serious injuries in respiratory arrest.[16] Doug Ross provides treatment and we learn that she fell off a ladder; as the emergency intensifies and the patient is taken up for emergency neurosurgery, the steadicam glides outside the trauma room, following a nurse, and picks up the arrival of a boy, David, and older sister, Mandy – the patient's children. The camera pivots around them to reveal an adjacent corridor as Carol Hathaway (Julianna Margulies) arrives to explain what is happening. We find out that the mother has been here before with serious injuries and Doug suspects her husband has been assaulting her. He talks to the children, asking, 'you want to tell me who's been hitting your mom for the last six months? She can't take a lot more of this ...' but they say nothing. As Doug goes to leave, the younger boy says, 'It was Mandy,' and Mandy begins to violently threaten and attack her brother until Doug separates them. As David asks, 'When can my mom come home?' the camera swings up to Doug's astonished face and the title sequence begins.[17] This sequence is notable for its remarkable choreography, with background visual planes full of patients, medical staff, beds being moved and phones ringing. We even get details reflected in the glass of the internal windows of the trauma room so that there is a sense of movement both in the background and in front of the frame, giving a dense concentration of movement and the implication of crowded and busy off-screen space, so that the layered textures of the title sequence are replicated in the *mise en scène* of the teaser and the rest of the episode. Textures in particular are important in establishing *ER*'s stylistic ambitions; it is a stylistic interest that is virtually absent from *Casualty*'s beginning which is much more interested in telling a story about the show.

Casualty regularly changes its title sequence and produces variations on its original musical theme tune. In its tenth season (1995–6) we begin with an electronic variation on the theme of ambulance sirens before the music builds to its main theme; visually we are offered a montage of various accidents taking place – falling down stairs at home, falling from scaffolding, sporting accidents, workplace accidents, car accidents and an assortment of shots with people in clear pain but with no apparent context. These shots are rendered in blue and further visual distortion is achieved by strobing the movement of the victims so that we get the sense of their calamity rather than its detail. The main musical theme begins with a shot of closing ambulance doors and the superimposition of a graphic grid within which various colour images of hospital care are seen: doctors treating patients, people on hospital beds being wheeled down corridors, etc; behind these we see the images, still behind a blue filter, of the journey of the ambulance along a motorway, down a side street and, as the music ends and the title 'Casualty' appears, the arrival of the ambulance at the hospital to be greeted by medical staff.

Unlike *ER* there is no sign here of characters or credits for characters and the only text visible is the ambulance sign and the title of the programme itself. There is also a clear narrative pattern: accident means ambulance means hospital care. The distorted siren sounds that we hear are pointedly juxtaposed with an image of the ambulance and its flashing lights so that there is little doubt about the relations between sound and image. (In *ER* the siren variations are a crucial part of the music but the ambulance is not visualised.)

Later seasons of *Casualty* stay with the idea that the title sequence should tell a story. The 2000–01 season foregrounds the importance of speed and urgency as aspects of emergency care, by crosscutting between the accelerated minute hand of a wall clock in the emergency treatment room, and point-of-view shots derived from the front of an ambulance, similarly speeded up. The ambulance's journey to and from an accident rendered in point-of-view style is extended to inhabit the interior of the hospital where we eventually (in-between clocks) see a bird's eye view of the accelerated treatment of a young black boy. There are some gestures towards textural juxtapositions, such as brief extreme close-ups of plasma bags and the oozing of blood along plastic, but these seem something of an afterthought and are subordinate to the main idea of the title,

'the ambulance's journey home': title
sequence from *Casualty*

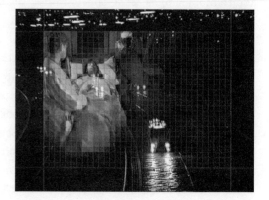

which is a simplistic visualisation of 'the race against time'. In each case a verbal idea – 'the race against time' or the 'story of the ambulance's journey home' is more or less directly translated into pictures.

Cardiac Arrest's title sequence is similar to both *ER* and *Casualty* in that it begins with a quiet synthesiser-produced sound that rises to a crescendo before the main theme starts. Alongside this ambient, rather haunting sound we see images of medical textures and objects melted into one another – a treatment room, an IV drip, a distorted surgeon's mask, an X-ray of a hand; the images are either being rotated or approached with a 'floating' camera movement which ends, as the main musical theme begins, at a set of double doors. From here on things get rather schematic: the camera's bursting through the doors sets off sirens and releases in a spin the stark title 'Cardiac Arrest' in red font against a white background (there is a hint of a red flashing light behind it, in case we missed the full significance of the juxtaposition). The subsequent image carries actors' credits, and is a slow-tracking shot along a white hospital corridor: again, visual distortion is achieved by strobing the image and using overexposure effects, so that the white décor of the hospital ward seems to glow and bleed over the objects within it. As in *ER*, the advantage here is in the use of textures and settings to suggest narrative and stylistic interests and tone, rather than to merely illustrate a narrative or single idea. However, the interest in textures and glimpses of technology in the first part means that the subsequent tracking shot carries comparatively little visual interest except as a backdrop onto which to hang the credits.

Chicago Hope is far more upbeat, and also splits its title sequence into two parts. Backed by electronic rhythms, the single horn that produces the main theme expresses 'all things hopeful', to a visual backing that is mixture of green textures and a medley of extracts at the service of character presentation. Unlike *ER* the extracts are eager to signal the friendship *between* characters as much as their common goal of healing the sick. The pace of the cutting between these clips is directly linked to the tempo of the music (which eventually produces an absurd rapidity). In-between these shots there is some repetition of the 'Chicago Hope' title, before the second half introduces the actor text credits, which are oddly superimposed over a what looks like a procession of faceless people walking along a corridor; it is difficult to tell because the sequence is distorted by textured green layers. These textures are then jettisoned in favour of a quick montage of scenes which pick up precise gestural moments of the main characters – removing glasses, looking up at a distraction – that are too brief to be of any significance (either separately or cumulatively). The final shot, which is very clear, is the 'badge of quality': 'Chicago Hope created by David E. Kelley' set against the background of a zipped-up body bag.

Gideon's Crossing inherits some of the style of its title sequence from that of *ER* in that it refuses narrative linearity and presents its main actors in a medley of shots. In its opening moments there is the same emphasis on medical and scientific objects and textures, with some suggestion that this is cutting-edge technology, so for example, we see the letters of the title formed from shapes similar to those on an illuminated DNA gel. As in *Chicago Hope*, a horn solo carries the main theme while we are shown character vignettes in a style that is strangely redolent of the *Dynasty* title sequence. Unlike the shots of characters in *ER* which actually tell us rather little about them, it is clear that Ben Gideon (Andre Braugher) is *the* central character. They also tell us that he is a teacher at a teaching hospital, that he is passionate and his passion is sometimes expressed as anger. The sequence ends with the sound of a female choir building to a crescendo, implying a spiritual dimension to that teaching and treatment; the final shot is of a black hand holding that of a newborn baby (white). Clearly, 'issues' are to be foregrounded in this show in a sensitive but stimulating manner. The figure of the doctor as a holy hero – or as God – has been continually questioned by medical dramas since at least *M*A*S*H* and *St Elsewhere* and probably before that. *Gideon's Crossing* makes the choice to revisit this figure to see if he can stand up against the pressures of relativism and the popular loss of faith in scientific progress.

Action and setting

The emergency room setting demanded a style that could rise to its natural status as a site for receiving the products of contingent and unexpected accidents and illnesses. As Alan Alda argues,

> I think if there is any advantage for an actor playing a doctor it's that you get handed to you situations in which the stakes are automatically higher. You're not arguing with your wife standing in the bedroom about not wanting to do the laundry anymore … Life is heightened.[18]

The new hospital shows offer the prospect of a sudden accident as part of their generic promise. As the creator of *Cardiac Arrest* commented, 'anything can walk through the door – although they don't often walk'.[19] Indeed, an important iconic feature was the routine depiction of a gurney laden with injured victim being pushed through the emergency room doors. The sudden arrival of an injured patient allowed rapid interruptions and changes in plot and character development, as the narrative space is invaded by the new dramatic component. There is sometimes the sense of conversations, disagreements and narrative developments being interrupted or cut off by the new emergency, with the treatment of injured patients reframing those narrative strands and conversations in relation to Alda's sense of 'higher stakes'.

One of the ways this happens is by intertwining medical emergencies with interpersonal conflict, so that acute personal and professional issues come to a head at the same time, usually over the treatment of a bleeding, dying patient. Ordinary and melodramatic events such as romantic desire and conflict, unfulfilled ambitions and competition between staff for promotion may be interrupted by the demands of emergency care where doctors have to negotiate between their professional duty and their emotions. For example, in *ER*'s second season emergency surgeon Peter Benton (Eriq LaSalle) and trainee doctor Jeanie Boulet (Gloria Reuben) begin an affair, but Boulet is married and admits she doesn't want to leave her husband. Benton ends the relationship but his resentment towards her is manifest during their working lives in the emergency room, and this begins to compromise their treatment of patients.[20] The drama is heightened because what is at stake is more than the survival of the patient (who we don't know well) but the reputation, moral security and professional ethos of the doctors (who we do know).

The hint of blood during some of the title sequences of the show signals their interest in body horror and visceral explicitness, and promises bloody spectacles as one part of the reward for viewing. Speed and visceral explicitness were, from the beginning, perceived as inheritances from the television crime fiction and horror movie genres as well as the emergent reality television shows. But whereas crime fiction's fast, urgent style was often an unmotivated and self-conscious exhibitionism (see *Homicide: Life on the Street* and *NYPD Blue*) that expressed the anxious, uncertain and risky spaces of police procedure, in hospital drama emergency medical attention is *ipso facto* speedy and immediate, and this provided the necessary realist permission for the adoption of an accelerated visual style. The speedy visual style seems to emerge 'naturally' from the dramatic setting of emergency care, where the camera reacts to or discovers events.

However, it would be wrong to classify new hospital dramas as unremittingly speedy and fast paced. Indeed it is one of the discoveries of Lars von Trier's hospital-based mini-series *Riget/The Kingdom* (1994) that the hospital could function as a setting for the gothic and the uncanny, depicted at a relatively slow pace. In mainstream hospital dramas the prevalence of action scenes is balanced by less frenetic moments of reflection, which are generally slower and dialogue-based. There is an alternation between these scenes of action and reflection that gives the new hospital dramas their narrative shape. Of course, dramatic narratives that mix 'action' and 'reflection' are not confined to television since they are common feature of literature, theatre, film and painting. However, I want to align new hospital dramas with forms like the Hollywood musical and pornographic films, among others, that clearly signal the distinction between narrative and number. This is not to claim that the two are mutually exclusive: as Linda Williams points out, 'Narrative informs number, and number, in turn, informs narrative'.[21] Similarly in hospital dramas the action mode does not signal the suspension of the narrative but invites the opportunity for conflicts to be created or resolved. Action sequences render a world where medical staff have to resort to a grid of rules in the face of the spontaneous unpredictability of the body's illness and injury. The division of medical labour is also visualised, conveying a framework of usually ordered medical care that is contrasted with the spontaneous and sometimes unanticipated response of the body to that treatment.

Typically, the change to action mode is motivated by the arrival of a new patient requiring urgent treatment, or the worsening of an existing case. In the transition to action mode, the medical dramas delight in foregrounding the radical contingency of accidents and the 'sudden turn for the worse' that can befall patients. Unlike the horror film, where moments of gore are carefully prepared for by sound, image and narrative, the 1990s medical drama profits from the realistic assumption that accidents can happen anywhere, anytime. As noted above, the sudden event of a gurney bursting through double swing-doors is the most familiar moment that signals the move into action mode.

The visual and aural layers of the programmes tend to become denser as they move into action mode, with the spaces of the corridor and trauma room mediated by a mobile camera or quick cutting so that changes of shot scale are rapid and fluid. Camera mobility in the long take may be combined with fast editing that switches between the various elements in the division of medical labour (patients, doctors, monitors, etc.). Extradiegetic music reinforces the sense of pace, and the dialogue becomes a fast exchange of instructions, observations and questions couched in a more or less opaque medic-babble, and the sounds of monitoring devices augment and punctuate the action. Shots rendered with low-key lighting are often contrasted with brightly lit shots of the injury sites and the details of suture, needle insertion and scalpel incision.

However, as the title sequences imply, alongside this sense of order there is also a sense of confusion and of panic near the surface. The speed of the depiction intensifies the unexpected – the body's ability to improvise complications – so that things rarely go to plan and the ever-present danger is that the doctors will run out of procedures before the body stops 'improvising'. This rhapsody of monitoring, insertion and invasion is intercut with the sharp sideways checking glances that the doctors and nurses exchange, their anxiety or confidence in what they are doing providing the basis for our response. Hence the process of treatment is matched in an economy of looking. The medical diagnostic gaze implies the doctors' mastery of the situation, but we are also aware that this may develop into a look of helpless compassion, horror, dread or morbid fascination. This economy of looking invites our alignment with the medical staff particularly when they are in control and when they are not.

Action mode: the division of medical labour and economy of looking in *ER*'s trauma room

One of the paradoxes of these scenes is that medical treatment generally means subjecting the body to invasive techniques. We are offered the body horror traditionally associated with the horror film genre, in the context of medical care. The doctors slice open and insert tubes into the traumatised body, electrocuting it in order to bring it back to health and life. 'I'm in!' signals a successful invasion of the body cavity that enables further care to be achieved; our proximity to the suffering of patients is therefore mediated by the seemingly odd pleasure that the doctors display when cutting and shocking patients. In Linda Williams's account of what she calls 'gross body genres' (melodrama, horror and pornography) she describes those sequences where the body is shown in the grip of uncontrollable spasms and involuntary 'bodily ecstasies' (for example, weeping, suffering, orgasm).[22] But in new hospital dramas the body is regulated (indeed the new hospital dramas seem to articulate Michel Foucault's ideas of the disciplined body), extended and technologised as a crucial part of the *mise en scène*. The heartbeat becomes the sound of the EKG monitor; blood is circulated through tubes, bags and ventilators assist breathing. The ruined body is dispersed through the technology of medical treatment and further dispersed through the looks and observations of the medical carers.

Unlike body horror movies such as *The Thing* (1982) where we see the transformation, slicing, invasion and exploration of the body cavity offered to us as horror spectacle, in *ER* and *Chicago Hope* such scenes became routinised and, to a certain extent, glamorised while maintaining an underlying aesthetic 'kick' of the visceral. But the meaning of such butchery that we see is firmly closed, directed to positive healing rather than violent destruction. One could say this aspect of the horror genre has found a mainstream audience because the meaning is framed in such a fashion. Importantly, it is within a dramatic context of medical care that stylised scenes of medical intervention into living body cavities becomes distinct from similar moments in the horror film.[23] In horror genre narrative depictions of wounding, bleeding and injury constitute the spectacular payoff, a reward for suspense and fear. At the beginning of *Scream* (Craven, 1996) for example, Casey

Becker (Drew Barrymore) is chased around her parents' home and eventually stabbed repeatedly in the abdomen by a serial killer. This final moment of bloodletting constitutes the climax of the suspenseful opening and offers a very disturbing 'reward' in its graphic depiction of fatal injury. However, medical dramas use the spectacle of injury as a marker on a longer narrative journey. The 'payoff' in this respect is not so much special effects and make-up, but the suspense generated around the possibility of healing the ruined body so that injury and treatment is the starting point of the drama, not its conclusion. Nevertheless there is a disturbing sense that the finality of the spectacles offered in horror movies are not available in medical drama – the body just goes 'on and on' as doctors and surgeons battle to heal it (see the extended discussion of 'Love's Labor Lost' in Chapter 5).

In the same way, the frequent visualisation of cardiopulmonary resuscitation (CPR) is both a familiar action scene in new hospital drama and one that can go on for the duration of an episode (it is not unusual to hear staff talking about the fact that it is thirty or forty minutes since the heart stopped). These begin when, at some point during treatment, the patient 'crashes' (has a cardiac arrest, signalled aurally by the electrocardiograph's shrill alarm); we then see attempts to revive the patient using electric shocks provided by the defibrillator paddles. As I noted in the introduction, visually there seems to be a contradiction since the patient's body is subjected to various forms of trauma in order to heal it: punching (cardiac massage), needle insertion (blood/plasma in vein, adrenaline), electrocution, and the possibility of open heart massage as a final resort (requiring a thoracotomy using 'rib-spreaders').[24] Sometimes CPR scenes are more about the display of the doctor's commitment to their patients and are usually a strong indicator of the doctor's investment in care. The depiction of cardiac arrest and the subsequent intensity of medical attention is inherently dramatic:

> Cardiopulmonary resuscitation is well suited to dramatisation, being visually interesting and conferring an atmosphere of urgency and excitement to a scene. ... In some instances, cardiopulmonary resuscitation seems to be used solely for its dramatic effect, without necessarily being important to the storyline or involving key characters, but creating the impression of a busy medical unit. For example, episodes of both *Cardiac Arrest* and *Casualty* opened with characters in the middle of an unsuccessful resuscitation sequence, thereby immediately creating an intense atmosphere and seizing the attention of the viewer. ... The atmosphere is highly charged, the activity is mesmerising, and the emotions and skills of the main characters are often tested to their limit and beyond. ... nowhere is the power of doctor-heroes over life and death so visible.[25]

As noted above, often we enter action scenes *in medias res*, with the patient already unconscious and being subjected to various intensities of medical treatment. For example, the following action sequence of *Cardiac Arrest* begins with a cut from a quiet dialogue-based scene to close shots of a patient's clothes being cut away with a razor, a body writhing, the sounds of a woman in pain, and the urgent beeping of an electrocardiograph.[26] Cut to close-ups (including partial faces of the rest of the medical team) of the anaesthetist James (Jo Dow) ('Oxygen running'), another doctor, Raj (Ahsen Bhatti) ('She's shutting down ... I can't find a vein anywhere') and the nurse, Julie, who calls out the history, 'Diane Lucas, thirty-one-year-old prima gravida, eight weeks pregnant. Pedestrian involved in an RTA [road traffic accident].' The senior doctor, Scissors (Peter O'Brien) tells the patient, 'I'm going to examine you. I'm sorry if you feel any discomfort, but it's not safe to give you painkillers in this condition.' On 'discomfort' we are offered a close shot of Diane in agony, her face partially obscured with an oxygen mask. There then follows a fast series of shots as Scissors issues instructions to the team, and verbalises his observations:

> *Scissors:* Raj get an IVI going ...
> *Julie:* Chest exposed, collar fixed.
> *Scissors:* Chest wall intact. No paradoxical movement.
> *James:* Can you take over the airway Julie? *[Diane is sobbing]*
> *Julie:* All right, Diane.
> *Scissors:* Probable haemothorax. *[Blood in chest cavity]*
> *James:* I can't get a vein anywhere. I'm going to do a central line.
> *Julie:* Steady!
> *Scissors:* Raj get a chest drain kit ready please. She's having contractions ... She's aborting.
> *[Raj stares between Diane's legs]* Come on Raj, help James with the central line.
> *Raj:* Sorry.
> *James:* Try and hold still. Sharp pain – won't last long.
> *Scissors:* Diane, I'm going to make a small incision in your side and insert a chest drain kit just to release the pressure around your lungs.
> *James:* Nearly over.
> *Scissors:* Here we go then, ready. *[Blood pours from her chest into a bottle]* Well done, that's the worst of it. ... Inserting ... I'm in! Clamp the tube and connect please.

The scene exemplifies the sense that the body in hospital drama 'improvises' its own destruction and therefore continues to present challenges to the medical staff. After the chest drain is inserted, James notices that 'Her belly's distended – something's ruptured in there,' and few moments later, 'She's losing consciousness – did anyone mention head injuries?' She is taken to surgery by a consultant surgeon where she is pronounced brain-dead, and becomes a candidate for organ-donation.

The constant sounds of Diane in increasing pain contrast with the more or less calm exchange of commands and observations between the medical team. But the choice of shots offers another sense to the obvious tragedy of the scene. Scissors is shot and lit from below giving him a slightly menacing air, and brief shots detail the movement of bodily fluids – blood rushing down a plastic tube into a bottle – gloved hands tapping the flesh searching for a vein, and the insertion of the chest drain tube is shown to us in brightly lit detail. We do not 'see' Diane's miscarriage, but we do see it being seen. It is signalled by a shot of a blanket pulled from across her broken legs, showing them covered in blood. At 'She's aborting', we get a shot of the junior doctor, Raj, looking down between Diane's legs; he appears shocked, fascinated and distracted by it. (It is worth comparing this to *ER*'s 'Love's Labor Lost' episode discussed in Chapter 5. The dramas raise the question of what is filmable – showable – while also implying off-screen spaces that are strongly gendered as well as abject.)

This scene has further narrative implications which, in part, explain its explicit use of a pregnant woman in pain. The driver of the car that injured the woman is in the hospital too, and he is evidently very drunk. He tells Scissors, 'I had a bit of a knees-up after work. I did a big deal today, made a lot of money.' Scissors examines him, finds something is wrong but nevertheless decides to pronounce the drunk driver OK: 'Nothing serious at all.' It transpires that the driver has a ruptured liver requiring urgent surgery, and we later learn that Scissors' murderous motivation is connected to the death of his wife, who was also killed by a drunk driver. Scissors' actions are therefore offered to us as part of the moral choice: we are asked to balance the drunk, obnoxious, white male who has made a lot of money against the pregnant woman who spent her last conscious minutes in horrific pain. The justification for the pain inflicted on the woman is located in the moral issues it raises for the doctor (do I treat her killer?) and, later, the husband, who Scissors asks for consent to use his wife's organs for transplant. Even in new hospital dramas extreme suffering and pain has to be mobilised in order to give moral weight to the doctor's decision to deliberately misdiagnose a patient.

In *Always and Everyone* we see an action sequence that carves its distinction by withholding some of the familiar generic features of the emergency action scene established by the new hospital dramas earlier in the decade. A young boy is brought into the emergency trauma room with breathing difficulties and he quickly loses consciousness. The music is urgent and develops a faster tempo as the difficulty in reviving the boy intensifies; there is rapid cutting between the medical staff who are trying to revive him and the boy's anxious mother. However, as soon as the boy's heart stops, the music is cut and the only sound we hear is the flat-line whine of the EKG monitor as the senior doctor administers CPR without resorting to defibrillation. The boy is revived without shocks or open heart massage in an example of the way a show can use generic expectations to craft novelty and surprise. This series often attempts to distinguish itself from the other members of the genre in this way; so for example, a sudden cut to a very gory (and narratively insignificant) open heart massage offers special effects dislocated from the narrative weight that would usually justify them.

A potent example of the action scene prompted by a patient's sudden 'turn for the worse' is *ER*'s 'Freak Show'.[27] The episode begins with Peter Benton (Eriq LaSalle) dressing for work near his locker; on the door he has a picture of his son, who was born very prematurely and is deaf. Peter has been estranged from him since he split up with the boy's mother. Soon after, a young black boy, Rodney, is rushed to the trauma room after being hit by a car. Peter's diagnosis of the child's injuries is complicated by the fact that the boy has a rare genetic disorder that means his abdominal organs are in the reverse position to normal. The injured boy becomes something of a biological celebrity with researchers crowded around the operating room using digital-camcorders and flash photography to record the phenomena. The abrasive head of surgery, Robert Romano (Paul McCrane) sees this as a great research and teaching opportunity. However, Benton realises the boy and his father reflect his own situation (the boy was with his father during the accident but normally lives with his mother). The proximity of the case to Benton's personal situation is further reinforced when the boy's father, Isaac (a black man strongly coded as working class), recognises Benton as a former high-school celebrity. Romano has instructed Benton to take a sample of the boy's and the father's blood so that they can research the possibilities of genetic inheritance. Isaac, unaware of his son's condition and impressed that 'All the doctors have been in to see him to make sure

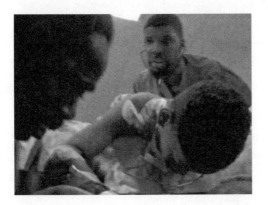

Peter Benton (Eriq LaSalle) attempts to save a child with a pulmonary haemorrhage in *ER*, 'Freak Show'

he's alright', gives his consent for blood to be drawn from the still unconscious boy in the mistaken belief that this is part of the treatment of his injuries.

By sheer coincidence, as Benton draws the blood Rodney's blood pressure drops dangerously low and he suffers a pulmonary haemorrhage, so that he begins to drown in his own blood. In an effort to help him breathe they turn him over on the table, blood pours from his mouth and the camera tilts down following the flow to the floor. Peter desperately tries to save the boy but after twenty minutes he is forced to stop and we see Isaac crouching near the table to lift and hold his dead son's bloodied arm. Later Benton asks Isaac for consent to do an autopsy but he cries, 'I don't want my boy's body studied,' and Peter backs off. Romano, absent from the harrowing scenes we and Peter have witnessed, demands that the boy's body is made available for study, 'Give him [the father] some time, he was emotional. How do you think we make advances? He was a freak of nature, we're scientists.' The vivid and disturbing action scene thus services several narrative functions. It allows Benton to clarify his moral commitment to the advancement of science in the light of his own fatherhood, and it closes the meaning of scientific medical research as inherently brutal and insensitive. Action scenes are far more potent when the doctors administering emergency treatment have a personal as well as a professional stake in the outcome: Peter's desperate struggle to save Rodney is of course a displacement of his own fears and concern for his son. In their action sequences then, new hospital dramas are frequently concerned to activate wider emotional and social issues that go beyond the spectacle of injury.

Notes

1. Dr Morganstern (William H. Macy), *ER*, 'Summer Run', season 2, episode 2 (1995).

2. *ER*, *passim*.

3. Jon Dovey, 'Reality TV', in Glen Creeber (ed.), *The Television Genre Book* (London: BFI, 2001), p. 135.

4. John Caldwell, *Televisuality: Style, Crisis and Authority in American Television* (New Brunswick, NJ: Rutgers University Press, 1995), pp. 284–301.

5. See José Arroyo (ed.), *Action/Spectacle Cinema* (London: BFI, 2000).

6. John O'Reilly, 'The real macabre', *The Guardian* (3 July 1995), p. 4.

7. Ibid.

8. Jim Shelley, 'Fatal attractions', *The Sunday Times* (13 September 1992), p. 8.

9. Ibid.

10. Jeremy Laurance, 'Video of surgery aims to shock rather than inform', *The Times* (28 August 1996). It was alleged that surgeons working in the NHS were paid to supply this footage; Jill Sherman, 'Surgeons were paid £1000 for videotapes of operations', *The Times* (27 August 1996).

11. Caldwell, *Televisuality*, p. 80.

12. Ibid., pp. 80–1.

13. V. F. Perkins, *The Magnificent Ambersons* (London: BFI, 1999), p. 54.

14. Jostein Gripsrud, *The Dynasty Years* (London: Routledge, 1995), pp. 183–4.

15. John Caldwell, 'Steadicam', in Horace Newcomb (ed.), *The Encyclopedia of Television*, vol. 3 (Chicago, IL: Fitzroy Dearborn, 1997).

16. *ER*, 'Long Day's Journey', season 1, episode 14 (1995).

17. Although this story is not developed and Doug's initial surprise changes to resignation when, after the title sequence, he tells medical student Chen that 'we see three or four of [such cases] a month'.

18. *Playing Doctor* (BBC, 1996).

19. Quoted in the *Radio Times* (15–21 April 1995), p. 86.

20. Benton ends the relationship in episode 3, 'See One, Do One, Teach One', but it is not until episode 6, 'Days Like This', that we see the two at work together; hence multi-narrative shows can plant narrative events whose consequences may not be felt until some time later.

21. Linda Williams, *Hard Core: Power, Pleasure, and the 'Frenzy of the Visible'* (London: Pandora Press, 1990), p. 130.

22. Linda Williams, 'Film Bodies: Gender, Genre, and Excess', *Film Quarterly*, vol. 44, no. 4, (Summer 1991), p. 4.

23. *The Thing* (1982) manages to combine both care and horror in a scene where a cardiac arrest victim transforms into the monster at the point of defibrillation. See also Joan Hawkin's *Cutting Edge: Art Horror and the Horrific Avant-garde* (Minneapolis: University of Minnesota Press, 2000).

24. The fact that the survival rate for cardiopulmonary resuscitation in British medical dramas holds at a realistic 25 per cent (compared to 77 per cent in *ER* and *Chicago Hope*, both of which use a disproportionate number of children in these situations) further suggests a downbeat tendency. See P. N. Gordon, S. Williamson and P. G. Lawler, 'As seen on TV: observational study of cardiopulmonary resuscitation in British television medical dramas', *British Medical Journal*, vol. 317 (19 September 1998), pp. 780–3.

25. Ibid., p. 782.

26. *Cardiac Arrest*, 'Breaking Strain', season 3, episode 12 (1996).

27. *ER*, 'Freak Show', season 4, episode 8 (1997).

3

'See One, Do One, Teach One': Learning to Be a Doctor

At the moment there are so many medical series and serials being aired that if you watch a cleverly planned selection, you will soon be able to conduct your own operations.[1]

Early on in the first episode of *ER* the junior doctor John Carter (Noah Wyle) is going through the motions of diagnosis with a patient complaining of chest pain; he hesitates and Susan Lewis (Sherry Stringfield) has to prompt him. The patient complains, 'Who is he – a beginner?' 'This is a teaching hospital,' explains Susan. All the hospitals in this study, with the exception of *Chicago Hope*, are teaching hospitals and therefore have a mixture of student doctors and teaching doctors. Reproducing the knowledge, methods and values of medicine is their primary professional aim in this context, but the dramatic aim of the show is to instruct the audience about the professional codes and particular medical procedures, as well as the genre itself. The audience is 'trained' by the drama to accustom themselves with 'how things work around here' – in the genre, in this show – in much the same way medical students have to be attuned and acculturated to the laws and community of the hospital they study in.

Obviously medical students like Carter learn on the job by observing and sometimes participating in those action sequences I described in the previous chapter. However, all staff have to learn appropriate behaviour according to their rank too and if junior doctors struggle with developing a bedside manner alongside a competent medical approach, their seniors must also learn how to teach effectively and how to manage their authority. The visualisation of teaching often takes place in moments outside the busy action sequences, moments of reflection that are mainly dialogue-based exchanges between senior and junior doctors (the failure to learn, however, is typically revealed in the action sequences). I use the word reflection to signal the way in which this mode provides the opportunity for characters to reflect upon and argue about the way things are done or have been done, so that characters might discuss the

Susan Lewis (Sherry Stringfield) and Doug Ross (George Clooney) discuss a patient in *ER*'s busy corridor

ramifications of an action scene. It is part of the negotiation between individuals in an institution with their colleagues and with their personal, private commitments. As Steve Bailey notes of the 'professional' television 'super genre':

> the professional figure operates within a larger institution and must continually negotiate the demands of such institutions … in the light of personal moral, financial, sexual, and physical needs. This tension exists between the 'individual' (in very much the classic, bourgeois sense) and the impersonal, often a bureaucratic institution occupies a central place in both diegetic and extradiegetic discourses.[2]

Reflection scenes in new hospital dramas extend a familiar moment in the wider category of television workplace drama, that are necessarily interested in dramatising the details of professional life, the explicit and implicit rules of the job, crudely, 'the way we work here'. Reflection modes can therefore be located in other examples of television fiction that are interested in the rhythms of professional life, particularly those that have a public function, and promise their own versions of 'action', such as police dramas, other emergency service dramas and those set in the legal profession.

Reflection scenes

These are dialogue-based moments of contemplation and have a strong pedagogical address, both internally (as characters receive training in medical skills) and externally (as the audience also has to learn 'the way things work around here'). The figure of the young trainee is a crucial component in the way audiences learn about the genre's specificity. A constant issue in new medical dramas is the difficulty in successfully reproducing medical skills and passing on wisdom from senior to junior staff. If the action mode is predicated on our fascination with the visceral, the reflection mode is interested in the way we talk about our lives, the way that rules govern and delimit our behaviour, and the ways in which the personal and the professional are intertwined.

The reflection scene can take place in the corridor, or more privately 'in my office' (in British shows like *Casualty* it is typically begun with 'in my office' for 'a word'), or less usually at home or in the recreation space. These are always about the negotiation of power relations between characters and this is frequently enriched by the conflation of professional and private lives (for example, a character is not doing his or her job competently because of a relationship problem). This mode relies on dialogue to shape its drama and is often stylistically nondescript, sometimes merely relaying stand-and-deliver performances. Shown in this way teaching and instruction is central so that we get a strong explication of the professional and interpersonal 'rules' of the hospital, and it is worth sketching out the permutations of these dialogue-based transactions. The most obvious form is the senior-junior conversation, the most common of what we might call the 'this is how we do things around here' conversation. Seniority in this case might mean explicit professional seniority – consultant/attending to house officer/resident – or seniority earned by duration of tenure or experience.[3] It is an explicit statement of the implicit rules of the working culture: how things are done (say, in medical procedure) and how things are done around here (in this hospital, in this programme). Take this example from the first episode of *Cardiac Arrest*.[4] The new house officer, Andrew Collin (Andrew Lancel), is called to administer his first CPR. It is a grim action sequence where we see Andrew lose the patient, and a reflection scene immediately follows:

> *Andrew:* I was just so utterly useless!
> *Claire:* Next time you won't be. You come out of medical school knowing bugger all – suddenly you're expected to cope with anything. It's no wonder August is the killing season. Newly qualified doctors hit the wards and the hospital mortality rates shoot sky-high. We all kill a few people while we're learning.

This exchange tells us two things. First, that *Cardiac Arrest*, the programme, is telling us about the real world (facts that are intended to shock us, part of the claim of the programme to show us 'how things really are'). Second, it tells us that Claire (Helen Baxendale) has been around long enough to distinguish the experiential truth from the 'official version'. It is therefore a double-range address telling Andrew and us the way things are – in his world and in the audience's world since the show takes the two to be congruent – and it is delivered by Helen Baxendale slightly turned towards camera as she is speaking. Hence the reflection mode can also function as an 'issues showcase', so that

'We all kill a few people while we're learning', Claire Maitland (Helen Baxendale) tells Andrew Collin (Andrew Lancel) in *Cardiac Arrest*

telling us about 'the way things work around here' is also telling us that new doctors kill people because their training is inadequate. Often the senior-junior exchange is an invitation for the junior member of staff to explain their shortcomings, often why personal circumstances have prevented them from doing their job properly. Hence the reflective scenes can explore the tension between maintaining the stability of professional procedure and a satisfactory personal life.

But if we reverse the order to junior-senior it is possible to think about another kind of exchange where junior staff challenge their seniors, perhaps catching them breaking the rules, or bending them to their own liking. In British medical dramas this often involves senior members being caught doing private practice to the neglect of their NHS work. What is crucial here is the discovered discrepancy between how things should be done (the official version) and actual, corrupt practice.

Another kind of exchange typical of reflection scenes is when workers of equal rank talk about their work so that we get junior-junior and senior-senior exchanges. As no one can 'pull rank' any conflict may be resolved by an appeal to more senior members of staff. Arguments between Susan Lewis and Mark Greene often have this quality of impasse. Conversely such exchanges may take the form of griping about the job, poor conditions, etc. There is also uncertainty because their knowledge is more or less equal: in the example of the 'Love's Labor Lost' (*ER*, see Chapter 5) the tension of the action sequences is augmented by the fact that all members of the team with equal seniority are equally at a loss as to how to proceed. Equally, senior-senior exchanges may also involve conflict about methods of management, teaching and appropriate healthcare.

In reflection scenes disagreements may often centre around two things. Medical students have to learn to be competent doctors, and often part of the dramatic potency of hospital dramas is watching the struggles to apply their knowledge in practice. However, it is not enough to learn how to fix an injured body. The dramas also demand that the doctors learn how to 'care' – how to exhibit sensitivity, politeness and compassion for their patients. For example, junior doctors are often brimming with care and compassion but lacking in the experience and training of how to administer competent treatment, and since they are not fully conversant with the professional code they often feel an affinity with the bewildered patients. Carter in *ER* is a good example of a student who begins the series full of compassion and sensitivity but, as he trains to become a surgeon, gradually abandons these traits in favour of a more cynical persona. Later he is convinced to return to ER medicine and adopt his previous persona. Junior doctors begin their careers medically 'incompetent' but basically 'good', in terms of their ready access to the display of their feelings and compassion for their patients. While their medical skills are lacking their interpersonal skills are in the right place: they have time for their patients. However, over-sensitivity can be a problem, with a concern for the patient's or their family's feelings overriding the provision of adequate care.

In the same way senior staff may well be professionally competent while lacking the interpersonal and compassion skills associated with good medical care. Adrian DeVries (Jack Fortune) in *Cardiac Arrest* is an example of this kind of figure, as is Kerry Weaver (Laura Innes) in *ER*. Typically the only way to break these hardened insensitive figures is to introduce a trauma so harrowing (usually with a child) that it causes them to break down, overwhelmed by emotion, abandoning the rigid professional code that is their justification for insensitivity. Competent doctors can therefore be 'bad' doctors and incompetent ones 'good'. Thus, doctors who can only relate to patients and one another on a procedural level are bad characters; those who offer authentic personal investment in what they are doing are good. The figure of the doctor who is technically competent but lacking emotionally is a generic favourite as is the reverse.

In *ER* the central teaching relationship is between John Carter and Peter Benton (Eriq LaSalle). Carter's destiny is to be educated, and his storylines almost always involve the juxtaposition of a medical and a romantic education, which can interact more or less strongly. Like the junior doctors in *Cardiac Arrest*, Carter is hesitant and uncertain about his future career, constantly agonising in the early seasons that his choice to specialise in surgery may be the wrong decision. His desire to be in on the action, to learn from experience often has comic consequences. When Benton allows Carter to scrub in on his surgery for the first time, he shows Carter how to scrub his fingers, wash his hands and put on his gown. However, as soon as Carter enters the operating theatre he contaminates himself by touching Benton and is forced to leave.

Benton too requires training – he is an excellent and ambitious young surgeon, but it is evident that he needs to soften his approach and exteriorise his feelings more often. He has technical ability without apparent compassion and the first season depicts how the overwhelming nature of his ambition compromises his relations with his family, in particular his sick mother. In a later season, the senior paediatric surgeon, Abby Keaton (Glenne Headly), teaches him to visualise the internal organs using touch alone – she teaches him literally how to *feel*: 'Don't break down into parts, see the whole' is her advice to him.[5] However, Benton's rigid and demanding teaching style has dire consequences when his harsh criticism of one of his students results in suicide.[6]

In the second season Carl Vucelich (Ron Rifkin), a leading cardio surgeon, adopts Benton as a research associate in order to help him with an apparently novel research project.[7] Like Raj in *Cardiac Arrest*, Benton is astonished at the luxury of senior professionals – he gets his own office and executive parking space, but there is a price to be paid. Later Vucelich invites him to his elegant dinner party where black servants serve the food and drink, while Vucelich rhapsodises about the value of medical science, 'medicine is a challenge, puzzles, impossibles'.[8] Later Benton discovers Vucelich has been doctoring his research results to exclude cases that do not fit his hypothesis, and challenges Vucelich at the risk of his career. Benton's integrity is discovered in such circumstances and his gradual softening is apparent after his son is born premature and deaf.

Learning to feel, to articulate compassion and sensitivity is one trajectory, but this can also be a source of danger to patients. After he suffers a serious heart attack the head of the ER, David Morganstern (William H. Macy) returns to work espousing a new perspective that 'every patient has a story'. (In contrast to his earlier comment, 'Give me a good sick body that needs a little slicing, and I'm a happy man.'). Unfortunately this new empathy for the patients comes at the cost of his competence – Morgenstern is so involved with their personal plight he makes fundamental errors in his surgery, and eventually retires.

Care and sensitivity are things that doctors can lose as well. After he is viciously assaulted, Mark Greene returns to work stressed and angry saying, 'it's not my job to be their [the patient's] best friend', an attitude that culminates in his shouting at a deaf woman, '[Your husband is] going to die!' underlined by a fast camera movement, from his to her face, like the arc of a scalpel. The entire ER ward is struck dumb and still by this, and Mark runs outside where he explains to the receptionist Cynthia (Mariska Hargitay) that he is 'losing control'. In a desperate act at reconnection with the world of sensation and feeling, he kisses Cynthia and they subsequently begin an awkward and doomed romance. The compensation for violence, tough working conditions and awkward patients is found in the unstable world of romance.

New hospital dramas draw on the conflict and uncertainty inherent in the training of doctors as a rich source of their drama, but it was *Cardiac Arrest* that first raised this as *the* central issue for the genre. I will explore this in more detail in the next section where *Cardiac Arrest* will be contextualised in relation to anxieties in the UK about the training of junior doctors.

Junior doctors in the UK

The ability to provide compassionate medicine was further compromised by the expansion of a new managerial culture in the British health service in the 1990s. The increase in managerial pressures and administrative organisation was seen as inimical to the practice of care.[9] One consequence of this was the failure to reproduce core values, as well as basic enthusiasm, in newly recruited doctors. By the late 1990s the *British Medical Journal* reported that there had been a reduction in applications for hospital posts, especially in general practice, and noted that many young doctors 'are highly critical and disaffected'.[10] In 1997 it was reported that junior doctors were alienated by this managerial culture that was 'eroding their ability to provide caring compassionate medicine'. According to the report junior doctors objected to being treated like 'proprietors of a pizza parlour to be called up at any time of the day and night' by the management.[11] The excessive hours worked by junior doctors were also seen as exploitative, their function to take up the slack of an NHS weakened by financial cuts. The obvious risk was that patient care was jeopardised by treatment by overworked junior doctors. A crude indicator of the way in which junior doctors' working hours became an issue is to look at the number of articles about the topic published in professional journals (such as the *British Medical Journal*). For the period 1971–88 there were six articles about junior hospital doctors; for 1989–97 there were twenty-six: the latter frequently include words such as 'stress' and 'disillusionment', and worry about the desertion rate of doctors leaving the profession. If nothing else, this suggests that junior doctors and their working practices had become a significant public and professional issue by the early 1990s.

A feature article in *The Guardian* in 1994 noted that, according to a British Medical Association survey, 'A quarter of those who remain in the profession now regret entering medicine. Half are suffering low morale and two thirds blame the Government's NHS reforms for widespread disaffection.'[12] The article includes an interview with Jed Mercurio, who was a junior doctor and the writer of *Cardiac Arrest*: 'I've lost count of the times I've tried to have a shit and been forced to go for some rapid, unhygienic, wiping process because I've had to run to a cardiac arrest.' He later describes himself as a 'cynical twisted bastard' and argues that 'if you've got the brains to be a doctor you ought to have the intelligence to realise you should be doing a different job'. The feature concludes by raising the question which forms the basis for *Cardiac Arrest*: 'Are our lives truly safe in the hands of callow 25-year-olds making life-and-death decisions after days without sleep?' At the time, the UK government had secured the exclusion of junior doctors from the European Union's Working Time Directive, and two coroners had recently cited 'junior doctor fatigue' as contributing to patient deaths. The government's 'New Deal' for junior doctors, setting a ceiling of seventy-two hours maximum per week, was seen as a way of avoiding paying overtime for extra work that was done anyway.

By the late 1990s disillusionment was recognised as a fact, rather than a whinge: as one junior doctor remarked on his experience of medicine, 'It's knocked every bit of enthusiasm right out of me. I'm at a massive crisis point – a great big crossroads. I feel I'd really like to give up ...' [13] The disillusionment was manifested in complaints about medicine's inflexible career structure, poor careers advice, 'lack of personal support systems and networks in medicine', poor working conditions and 'professional isolation', and a 'hostile, intrusive and aggressive' management culture. [14]

In 1997 the Policy Studies Institute published *Choosing Tomorrow's Doctors*, a study based on focus group interviews with junior and senior doctors. [15] The study was initiated in response to the recognition by the British Medical Association of the widespread complaints of doctors about their working conditions in the newly modified NHS. The study reported that young doctors were increasingly unhappy with their workload, over-burdened with responsibility and lacked confidence in what they were doing. Even advances in medical technology were perceived as a problem by the doctors because they added to work pressure and raised unrealistic, high expectations in the patients.

The response to the report indicated a shift in attitude to medical care, as can be seen in the following comment that questioned the wisdom of recruiting academic high-flyers as medical students:

> It may seem comforting to know that those who will hold our lives in their hands are the brainiest in the land. The field of medicine is now so vast, and the pace of advance so rapid, that only the best minds have a chance of acquiring the necessary expertise. But there is more to medicine than making a diagnosis. It is also about listening, understanding and providing reassurance based on secure knowledge – the soothing hand on the brow. [16]

The article goes on to cite the importance of the 'intuitive ear and bedside manner'. Implicit in this is that academic strength and compassion are, in some undefined way, incompatible, or at least not often found together. There is also an anxiety about the reproduction of appropriate skills. This is the 'bedside manner' problem, or more cynically, a public relations issue in a health service that positions its patients in a consumer-with-rights role. These compassionate qualities have been traditionally associated more with nursing and parenting than with medical professionals, but are a common generic feature of hospital dramas old and new, since the softening of characters is a good source of drama (see Peter Benton in *ER*). However, the *Choosing Tomorrow's Doctors* study revealed that many doctors did not like their patients; as one junior argued, 'Medicine was OK except for the people. I found the whole thing of having to look after people too difficult. I felt I couldn't do them any good – and I didn't give a damn anyway.'

One way to resolve this impasse between the demands of the job and requirement to exhibit care is in the world of ideas. In 1998 a careers handbook for doctors begins with a chapter entitled 'Post-modern influences'. It argues that for those members of 'Generation X',

> work alone would no longer provide the ultimate meaning in life. ... Instead, it would complement relationships with friends and family, as well as fitting in to a larger philosophical framework. For many, this framework would have a post-modern feel to it.[17]

Adopting the post-modern scepticism towards 'grand narratives' (in this case meaning progressive career structures, rationality and medical science) it welcomes the prospect of complementary medicine, fractured careers divided between home and family, leisure, an acceptance that doctor-patient power relationships are fraught with mistrust and suspicion (it quotes Coupland, Lyotard, Foucault and Cixous in support of these claims). The solution to disillusionment is to lower expectations. According to the handbook, the fundamental value that doctors should espouse is holism rather than materialism:

> To have enough is enough and the drive toward greater acquisition and status is not well developed ... Such a post-materialist worldview fits the idea of a mosaic society, in which networking and stakeholding predominate. It is the world of the corner shop and the bicycle, rather than the superstore and the two-car household.[18]

These ideas circulating and developing in the material world had already been articulated in television hospital dramas in the mid-1990s. Indeed, I have a strong sense that they anticipated ideas that were subsequently articulated in policy papers and textbooks such as these. The rejection of material rewards and concentration on the appeal of community (rather than networking) was an important aspect of the new hospital dramas. *Cardiac Arrest* was the first new hospital drama; it began in April 1994 in the UK (six months before *ER* and *Chicago Hope*). It was a fast-paced half-hour show that ran for three seasons, and was significant because alongside the fast pace, stylised visuals and graphic explicitness, it sought to provide an experiential account of the nation's failure to adequately train junior doctors. In some respects it offered a narrativised version of the political and policy anxieties that were in circulation at the time. In order to understand this conjunction of politics and TV drama I want to examine the origins, authorship, production and thematic design of *Cardiac Arrest* in some detail.

Cardiac Arrest: 'Flip but deadly serious hospital drama series'

Cardiac Arrest was set in a provincial district general hospital and was very successful, attracting about 8 million viewers per episode and lasting for three seasons. Previewing the first episode, 'Welcome to the House of Pain', the BBC's television and radio listings magazine noted that it was 'filmed in an almost documentary style, the series portrays what it is to be like a junior doctor in an unsentimental way including some of the blacker aspects of hospital life'.[19] Its production history is interesting since it demonstrates how the development of the genre can be a product of largely individual aspirations responding to socio-cultural pressures.

In 1993 a UK independent production company, Island World Productions,[20] responsible for such diverse and successful dramas as *Between the Lines* and *Ballykissangel*, placed an advertisement in the *British Medical Journal* asking for doctors with an interest in writing a situation comedy about general practice. The recruitment criteria did not require a track record in television writing, but instead emphasised the importance of direct experience in the medical profession. This was part of the Island World's strategy to badge the show with the authenticity of experience and attitude (while presumably using the sitcom format to dilute its potential criticisms of the NHS). But why was experience in the field of medicine more important than experience in television writing? One answer is in the traditions of British television drama since the 1960s.

The head of Island World was Tony Garnett, a veteran British television drama producer who had a reputation for making progressive television, largely established in his work as producer for the Ken Loach drama documentaries of the 1960s and 70s. He spent most of the 1980s working in Hollywood before returning to the UK to make shows such as *Between the Lines* which continued a tradition, more or less established by Garnett himself, of hard-hitting, realist engagement with contemporary national issues.

However, this was part of a wider tradition of British television that aligned realism with the authentic experiences of the writer. This has its origins in the beginning of commercial television in the UK in 1955 and the recruitment of regional writers (such as Alun Owen) by Sydney Newman for his *Armchair Theatre* anthology drama series.[21] The idea that writers should write about what they know is now a cliché, but it was taken seriously by those starting to write television drama in the 1950s and 60s, who wanted to expand the dramatic canvas that had hitherto been largely confined to classics, adaptations and London-based drawing-room dramas.[22] The emergence of the UK New Left in the 1960s, with its insistent (and rather puritanical) radical individualism similarly privileged the authenticity of experience as a political record. Scholars such as Raymond Williams and Richard Hoggart used their experience as the basis for many of their cultural analyses, and many feminist scholars in the 1970s and 80s similarly drew on their experience and foregrounded themselves in their research. 'Write about what you know' became the mantra of radical television drama in the 1960s and Garnett was central to its development.

Garnett is on record in the early 1970s endorsing the value of television drama that is based on commitment to express an attitude or opinion:[23] indeed, for Garnett solid experience was a key component in that drama's assertion of realism and authenticity. He argued that the previous generation of dramatists had an idealist philosophy,

> It was all in their heads, or at least in the TV studio. And if somebody pointed out that what they were doing was not remotely like the real world or anybody's real experience, they would say, 'We're doing Art'. We were very firmly not doing art, right? We were trying to make sense of the world.[24]

This anti-aesthetic aesthetic was restated by Garnett in the 1990s, although he acknowledged that one perspective was necessarily restricted:

> our job should be to tell *our* truth, to bear witness, whether through a situation comedy, a news programme or a drama. ... But my truth or anyone's truth is partial, in both senses of the word, so we need a whole range of truths on television all the time.[25]

It is clear that what Garnett was hoping to find on his return to Britain was not so much a radical politics as a radical *attitude*, a rebellious persona.[26] He recollects that he returned to discover a generation of television workers blighted by the 1980s:

> When I came back to television in this country at the end of the eighties, after

being away for ten years, I was faced with a generation that seemed to me to be cowed. I was hoping that people much younger than me would be storming up to my office, telling me that what I had been doing was a load of crap, and saying that *this* is what ought to be made and *this* is how we want to make it. But that didn't happen. Instead a lot of people came to see me with the air of the child who wants to see in the teacher's face what the right answer is, so that they could please and be accepted. Maybe this is what the 1980s did to that generation. You could tell that all they wanted was a job or a commission. They didn't come in with a raging passion, political or otherwise for a way of doing things that was different. That was seriously disappointing to me.[27]

Faced with his disappointment Garnett was eager to adopt a parental role:

I spend a lot of my time trying to find talented people. They don't need to know how to write a screenplay. If someone can create a believable world and the characters come off the page, they can be taught the rest. Part of what I do now with a generation growing up is try to create a secure atmosphere for them. *I'll* fight the broadcasters if necessary and I'll try to create a secure environment where I can *love* good work out of people.[28]

In this context it is not difficult to see why the contract for the medical sitcom was awarded to Jed Mercurio, a practising NHS junior doctor with no experience of writing for television. In an interview in the *Radio Times*, Mercurio at once rejected the sitcom idea and went about stamping his own attitude over the project:

I thought ... that it would be better to do a hard-hitting drama about junior doctors – with lots of laughs – instead of a sitcom. So, in *Cardiac Arrest*, patients are portrayed as doctors see them, not as patients see themselves. It's unashamedly biased. And unashamedly jaundiced.[29]

He situates his series as one that innovates in terms of bias and partiality, where his individual perspective is dispersed and sharpened across an ensemble cast, rather than using that cast to explore diverse views. In doing so Mercurio was consciously 'genre busting' in concentrating the thematic development around one clearly defined group: 'in *Casualty* what you see are the workings of a department. In *Cardiac Arrest*, even the nurses are seen from the junior doctor's perspective.' As always, the appeal to a sharper verisimilitude was part of the rhetoric, with Mercurio claming that, 'doctors in *Casualty* and *Surgical Spirit* don't talk like doctors'. A radical, angry attitude was also one that avoided politics:

'This series is intentionally apolitical ... there are elements which will provoke argument and discussion, and people who don't feel as I do might wish to contest the problems I portray.'[30]

The *Radio Times* made much of the fact that Mercurio wrote the first season of *Cardiac Arrest* in-between fifty-six-hour shifts as a senior house officer in a Wolverhampton hospital. Mercurio's cynicism was directed as much at the representation of doctors in hospital dramas as it was at the profession in real life. He cites the impact of film and TV representations of doctors on the popular imagination and his resentment of those promoting a positive cultural image of medicine:

> My nights on call are haunted by the image of Dirk Bogarde as Dr Simon Sparrow ... I can't help but be resentful of those halcyon days, when my own fitful on-call coma is disturbed by the half-hour staccato tune of a bleep.
>
> The television myth of the doctor continues, albeit in a slowly evolving form. Now that the fictional image is accepted as truth, it has become all the harder to challenge. In 1872 Eadweard Muybridge's photography proved that artists' representation of horses galloping with all four legs outstretched are inaccurate. When painters applied this new knowledge, complaints abounded that the pictures looked wrong. The reciprocal causality of life and art may hinder acceptance of a more truthful version of hospital life. But viewers are not the only ones who might prefer to cling on to the myth. I don't know many doctors who wouldn't want to step out of their miserable circumstances into any one of the more comfortable environments that television has created.[31]

In settling scores with both the history of the genre and with the medical establishment, Mercurio claimed to avoid overt political posturing (although he wrote the series under the alias John MacUre). If we return to the models of senior-junior transactions it is possible to see how the presentation of the programme itself occupies a 'senior', genre-educative position in relation to the (junior) audience. Interviews, such as those with Mercurio in the *Radio Times*, help delimit the generic boundaries, and prepare the audience for its mode of address.

The first series was set in the Crippen Ward[32] in a provincial general hospital, and followed the new house officer, Andrew Collin, as he encountered the brutal reality of the work. The second and third series were based in a casualty ward where the junior doctors of the first series were now senior house officers, themselves training the new graduate doctors. So, in subsequent series the failure of training is taken a stage further so that, in series two, the next new house officer, Phil Kirkby (Andrew Clover), experiences many of the same problems as Andrew, compounded by the fact that his teachers are only a year above the junior level themselves.

Cardiac Arrest's generic distinction was also constituted in relation to its generic contemporaries such as *Casualty* and *Peak Practice* (1993–), which did not indulge in the same oppressive cynicism. According to Mercurio:

> I think it was good that we had those programmes to contrast with – they distinguished us. We were really distinctive compared to them, we were the only one that injected a constant cynicism that permeated the series without any redemptive payoff – in other programmes doctors can be pissed-off but they see a baby born and are cured of their malaise. *Cardiac Arrest* was a reaction to these shows, it was very angry. And it was really a reaction to the smugness of other programme-makers who talked about how realistic their programmes were, but who didn't have a fucking clue.[33]

Mercurio demonstrated considerable skill and ability in steering Garnett and Island World away from the sitcom idea to something that basically allowed him to develop very sophisticated ideas about television characterisation in relation to genre and deepen the nihilistic edge of the series. The obvious past antecedents are *The Nation's Health* and the dark comedy, *The Houseman's Tale* (BBC, 1987; about indifferent and hungover medical staff), but neither of those get anywhere near the levels of sheer bitterness exhibited in *Cardiac Arrest*. The radical nature of the show's cynical rhetoric was recognised by the critics, but they complained that its argument was not clearly stated, and that some of the show was anachronistic. John Naughton noted that the consultants in *Cardiac Arrest* were portrayed like 'linear developments from *Doctor in the House* and James Robertson Justice'.[34] Polly Toynbee complained that the series had a radical form but no evidence of content: 'perhaps it could be useful polemic, but what for? More money for the NHS? Abolition of managers?'[35] Toynbee is right, but wrong to feel bothered by this: *Cardiac Arrest* did identify problems rather than offer solutions, but that was the point. It attempted to articulate a generational attitude that was unsatisfied with a traditionally solid middle-class career destiny. What was unusual about *Cardiac Arrest* was its partisan alignment with young junior doctors (most of the cast were in their early twenties), so that the experience of junior doctors' disillusionment is central. This shift from a critique of the health service in general, to one that is based on the working lives of a small group can be illustrated by comparing *Cardiac Arrest* to *The Nation's Health*.

The Nation's Health dramatises two issues: the macho culture of senior (male) doctors (wearing striped shirts and interested in getting rich through private practice), and the impact of privatisation 'by the back door'. Lack of beds, the pernicious influence of drug companies, and the discrepancy between private capital and personal welfare were common themes. The series also makes much of the insensitivity of doctors to patients' needs in terms of their lack of interpersonal skills, such as keeping patients in the dark about their illness and its treatment 'for their own good': the doctors do not treat their patients as people, but as vehicles for disease, as cases. *Cardiac Arrest* offers a similar criticism except that those badly treated are not the patients (although they might suffer as a result) but junior medical staff, overburdened and under-trained by consultants happier to canvass more lucrative private treatment.

In episode two of *The Nation's Health*, 'Decline', we see a consultant surgeon diagnose a case of fibroids, subsequently informing the patient that, as the problem is non-urgent, she will have wait months for an operation; she complains that she wants the operation as soon as possible and the consultant responds: 'What happens on the NHS is that you have to wait in line ... Were you to consult me privately – which I'm not advising of course – I can see you on Thursday.'

Over a decade later *Cardiac Arrest* repeats this example but in another context – the supervision and training of junior doctors. Andrew Collin, faced with the necessity of performing a complex procedure late at night, telephones his supervising consultant, Graham Turner:

> *Andrew:* I'm afraid I've only ever seen it done once.
> *Turner: [off-screen]* Then you've seen it.
> *Andrew:* But Claire's not on call tonight and, er, I'd feel more confident if you were supervising this procedure.
> *Turner:* Have a go, you'll be fine. *[Andrew puts down the phone; cut to Turner's office. He is speaking to a couple]*
> *Turner:* Forgive me. Clearly a three-month waiting list is intolerable, but privately this is something we can do next week.

Andrew proceeds with the treatment nervously ('I need the ... um ...' *Nurse*: The wire?) and he is eventually forced to call Claire, who, although she arrives drunk, still manages to complete the procedure successfully. In the ensuing conversation Andrew complains about Turner's behaviour (and refers to a previous incident where Turner's absence, causing a patient's death, was blamed on another junior doctor) and suggests he will make a complaint. Claire is pragmatic, 'Challenge the consultant's right to do private practice when he should be here? There's a hurricane in Florida; why don't you go over there for a piss instead?' Nevertheless Andrew decides to complain, until he realises (in a catch-22 moment) that the complaints procedure requires him to complain at first to his designated consultant who is, inevitably, Graham Turner.

The discrepancy between those young doctors working in a busy NHS ward and consultants who spend their time treating private cases is illustrated in an episode where Raj (Ahsen Bhatti) is punished for damaging the Jaguar of a senior surgical consultant (Adrian DeVries played by Jack Fortune). As Raj cannot afford to pay for repairs, DeVries suggests that Raj take over some of his private ward duties. When Raj arrives in the ward he discovers a fairy-tale world of friendly patients and nurses, room service, mini-bar, cable television and a video library ('Have you seen *Jurassic Park*?' asks one of the nurses, Raj replies, 'I work in it.')

However, not all senior doctors in *Cardiac Arrest* are part of this culture. Graham Turner is a monstrous version of the bad father: he is interested in his private practice and in treating young juniors favourably only to the extent that he recognises his own background in them. Adrian DeVries's failings are similar – public school background, interest in private practice and material trophies – his Jaguar, his mistresses, smart clothes and haircut. Doctors of comparable rank to Turner and DeVries, but who do fulfil their roles as teacher and trainers (such as Barry Yates [Fred Pearson] and Ernest Docherty [Tom Watson]) provide a balance. As Yates says, 'I remember a long time ago when the most important people were the patients,' and he reassures a new junior doctor that 'My bleeper's always on,' offering the promise of nurturing availability (the bleeper is a source of complaint among the junior doctors). It is their distance from aspirations to financial or material rewards that distinguishes the junior doctors, an implicit signal that they are not corruptible. Similarly, in *ER* Mark Greene's goodness is established, in part, because he rejected his wife's suggestion of moving to a lucrative private practice.

Cardiac Arrest also dramatises the impact of 'clipboard culture' on the junior doctors. The hospital manager, Paul Tennant (Nick Palliser) makes his first appearance in the hospital posing as a wheelchair user, and discovers that most medical staff are too busy to direct him to the disabled toilets. He confronts Turner in a very busy ward with the rather piquant observation 'that the facilities here for the disabled are appalling'. Tennant is the epitome of the narrow-minded, nasty management culture, concerned about 'our image in the community'; his 'care' for his staff takes on a quite different meaning (as care for the disabled becomes an administrative weapon). The proliferation of management personnel is captured by staff nurse Julie Novac (Jacquetta May) who asks Tennant's secretary, 'I've been asked to see the hospital manager. Now would that be the clinical director, the business manager, the administrator, the administrative assistant, the unit manager, the assistant general manager, the executive or the chief executive, do you think?'

Cardiac Arrest describes a world where the reproduction of values is blocked because the rules and attitudes of the previous generation of doctors are corrupt and pernicious. Left with few convincing figures of compassionate and competent authority the junior doctors have to struggle against the forces of administration and patronage all by themselves. In retrospect Garnett's desire to nurture young writers with attitude paid off handsomely; Mercurio's achievement was to identify some of the central themes of the under-thirties generation at the time (themes subsequently taken up in shows like *This Life* and *Queer as Folk*). Although *Cardiac Arrest* pushed its concern with 'issues' in a traditional social realist sense each episode was also a showcase for emergent directorial talents (Audrey Cooke, Peter Mullan, Jo Johnson), and many were heavily stylised, quite unlike the unremarkable visual style of *The Nation's Health*.

Notes

1. Jan Moir, 'Oh, what a lovely ward!', *The Observer* (11 February 1996), p. 18.

2. Steve Bailey, '"Professional Television": Three (Super) Texts and a (Super) Genre', *The Velvet Light Trap*, no. 47 (Spring 2001), p. 47.

3. In the UK, medical students begin their practical training in hospitals as a house officer, then senior house officer, registrar, consultant. The US system uses a different terminology: intern, resident, attending (the latter usually supervises the teaching).

4. 'Welcome to the House of Pain', *Cardiac Arrest*, season 1, episode 1 (1994).

5. 'The Healers', season 2, episode 16 (1996).

6. 'Night Shift', season 3, episode 11 (1997).

7. 'Dead of Winter', season 2, episode 11 (1996).

8. 'True Lies', season 2, episode 12 (1996).

9. Jeremy Laurance, 'Young doctors alienated by clipboard culture NHS', *The Independent* (22 April 1997).

10. Peter Richard, Chris McManus and Isobel Allen, 'British doctors are not disappearing', *British Medical Journal*, no. 314 (31 May 1997), p. 1567. This has been challenged.

11. Laurance, 'Young doctors alienated by clipboard culture NHS'.

12. *The Guardian*, Weekend section (11 June 1994), pp. 6–13.

13. Isobel Allen, 'What Doctors Want from their Careers', in Isobel Allen *et al*. (eds), *Choosing Tomorrow's Doctors* (London: Policy Studies Institute, 1997), p. 29.

14. Isobel Allen, 'What doctors want', in Jamie Harrison and Tim van Zwanenberg (eds), *GP Tomorrow* (Abingdon: Radcliffe Medical Press, 1998), p. 145.

15. Allen *et al*. (eds), *Choosing Tomorrow's Doctors*.

16. Jeremy Laurance, 'Doctor, doctor, you're not on my wavelength: medical schools must

accept lower A-levels in order to avoid creating bored GPs', *The Independent* (20 August 1997).

17. Jamie Harrison, 'Post-modern influences', in Jamie Harrison and Tim van Zwanenberg (eds), *GP Tomorrow* (Abingdon: Radcliffe Medical Press, 1998), p. 4.

18. Ibid., p. 10.

19. *Radio Times* (16–22 April 1994), p. 86.

20. Island World Productions was run by Tony Garnett and Margaret Matheson; after the first season of *Cardiac Arrest* Matheson left and the company was renamed Island World.

21. See Glen Creeber, *Dennis Potter: Between Two Worlds* (Houndmills: Macmillan, 1998), pp. 38–9.

22. See Jason Jacobs, *The Intimate Screen: Early Television Drama* (Oxford: Oxford University Press, 2000).

23. Garnett: 'We wanted to find a new kind of writer. To do that you read everything. And invited people who'd never written anything before, perhaps, but who seemed to have something to say.' Quoted in Roger Hudson, 'Television in Britain: Description and Dissent', *Theatre Quarterly*, vol. 2, no. 6 (April–June 1972), p. 19.

24. Quoted in Hudson, 'Television in Britain: Description and Dissent', pp. 19–20. By the late 1990s Garnett argued that 'most television drama is the exploration of the human face. In fact most *television* is about exploring the human face ...' – precisely the claim that early TV drama directors made. Pat Holland, *The Television Handbook* (London: Routledge, 1997), p. 134.

25. Quoted in ibid., p. 132.

26. 'So what is Left? ... Capital has whipped labour's ass, the Unions are neutered and the Liberal Democrats are conspicuously to the Left of the Labour Party. In fact, some Tory MPs of my youth would find Labour now too right wing for their delicate consciences ... Frankly, there's not much Left ... The Left must begin again. Let's hope it does so facing this amazing future, not repeating and living in the past.' Tony Garnett, Raymond Williams Memorial Lecture, Birmingham, 1996.

27. Quoted in Holland, *The Television Handbook*, pp. 133–4.

28. Ibid., p. 134.

29. Quoted in Richard Johnson, 'What seems to be the trouble?', *Radio Times* (16–22 April 1994), p. 42.

30. Quoted in the *Radio Times* (28 May–3 June 1994), p. 98.

31. John MacUre (Jed Mercurio), 'Cold turkey for television's medics', *The Observer* (17 April 1994).

32. The infamous Dr Hawley Crippen was hanged for the murder of his wife.

33. Jed Mercurio interview with Jason Jacobs, 22 July 1997.

34. John Naughton, 'Slick operation with sick jokes', *The Observer* (24 April 1994), p. 25.

35. Polly Toynbee, *Radio Times* (22–8 April 1995), p. 14.

4

Men, Women and Patients

The concentration on the workplace as the site of professional and personal rewards replaced the domestic setting as 'home' in new hospital dramas. Frequently, characters with romantic and marital ties to home found these traditional relationships under strain, and the attractions of immediate colleagues more compelling. This chapter delineates the figuring of men and woman as modern types in the hospital drama and contrasts them to the presentation of the patients, who more often than not function as catalysts for character development.

Women

Until relatively recently women in medical roles have been represented in unfavourable terms: where they were not romantic fodder for male doctors' desires, they were emptied of their traditional feminine traits, becoming monstrous reversals of nurturing carers. Nurse Mildred Ratched (Louise Fletcher) in *One Flew Over the Cuckoo's Nest* (Forman, 1975) and the Nurse (Barbara Baxley) who tends to Cal's (James Dean) dying father at the end of *East of Eden* (Kazan, 1955) are memorable examples of monstrous 'carers'. In the latter film, the discovery of Cal's affection and love for his father is expressed precisely in his rejection ('Get Out!') of this uncaring figure, who is shown to be merely concerned with her own comfort and income. They embody a self-interest that is framed by a rigid adherence to rules and regulations that constrain natural expressions of care and freedom. Comic versions of the figure are common too, with Margaret 'Hot Lips' Houlihan (Loretta Swit) in *M*A*S*H* and Hattie Jacques's various incarnations of 'Matron' in the *Carry On* comedy films.[1]

Such representations seem unable to reconcile the fact that as medical carers such women professionalise their traditional feminine roles as nurturers, carers and healers. Unless the woman is figured as an explicit erotic object (young nurse in uniform), her femininity is figured as a monstrous abdication of her 'natural' instincts, in favour of medical codes of practice. If nurturing and caring is seen as a natural role for women, once it is professionalised – once these traits wear a uniform – they become problematic. Care is now at a price, part of the woman's self-development, not a given function of being a woman. At best this was a compromise, at worst a perversion.[2]

The refiguring of women medical staff begins in the 1970s when the 'conflict model' of medical care dominated television dramas, and the impact of feminism began to be articulated within them. The development of *M*A*S*H*'s 'Hot Lips' Houlihan from authoritarian sex object to a three-dimensional complex figure was indicative of these changes, as was the relative success of Paula Milne's nurse-centred series *Angels*. However, the positive articulation of feminist concerns was less evident than the critique of healthcare provision seen as corrupted by excessive and exclusionary masculinity and that provides the background to the increasing visibility of women doctors. The beginnings of this critique and the alignment of viewpoint with the perspective of a woman is evident in G. F. Newman's *The Nation's Health*, a four-part drama which centres around the early medical career and eventual disillusionment of Jessie Marvill (Vivienne Ritchie), who is a witness to malpractice, corruption and the terrible wages of chronic under-funding in the UK National Health Service. Most of the problems we see, however, are linked more or less explicitly to the arrogant 'macho culture' of doctors and surgeons. For example, we see a routine operation for the removal of fibroids (intercut with real surgical footage) where the surgeons discuss their leisure and business plans; one of them notices what seems to be a malignant tumour, and advises that they take the whole 'box' out. The juxtaposition of a casual discussion of masculine pursuits with the removal of the woman's womb has rich symbolic potency. However, since Newman's polemic is concerned to assert the necessity of militant trade unionism as a counter to the decline of the NHS, it is ambivalent as to the extent to which macho culture is a symptom or a cause of the problems. Jessie herself ends up isolated and alone by the end of the series.

By the 1990s the critique of masculinity was one of the most dramatised themes in all television genres. This developed in tandem with the routine visibility of female doctors in major roles established by *St Elsewhere* and *Casualty*. Charlotte Brunsdon in her discussion of television crime fiction in the 1990s notes various manifestations of 'the Equal Opportunities discourse' in that genre, where casting policy and narrative attention acknowledged the increasing entry of women in the professional working world.[3] While it is tempting to see a similar process at work in the hospital dramas of the 1990s, there are significant differences. Women figured as law enforcers have to occupy a traditionally masculine sphere; in medical drama the divide between the rejection of tradition and the innovation of female visibility in senior roles, is less clear cut, since the discursive context of new medical dramas places a high value on what are in fact traditionally feminine characteristics: care and nurturing, the very disavowal of which is a necessity in early 'Equal Opps' crime genres such as *Prime Suspect*. However, this is not to downplay the significance of women figures adopting medical roles that also favour the benefits of medical-scientific competency over intuition. A key character in this respect is Dana Scully (Gillian Anderson) in *The X-Files* (Fox, 1993–) who neatly combines the figure of law enforcer, medical scientist and rational sceptic (at least in the early seasons of the show). The suppression of traditionally feminine competences, such as sensitivity, intuition, care and the ability to build a home and nurture a family may promote success for women in other workplace genres (at the cost of domestic happiness), but the similar suppression of those features in medical drama affects the competency of the doctors themselves. In the world of the therapeutic state doctors have to be compassionate and caring, or they are coded as incompetent or dangerous.

In 1996 the cover of the BBC's television listings magazine carried the caption 'Docs in frocks: the rise of TV's medicine women' under a picture of Claire Maitland (Helen Baxendale) from *Cardiac Arrest*, Dana Scully (Gillian Anderson) from *The X-Files* and Samantha Ryan (Amanda Burton) from *Silent Witness* (BBC, 1996–2001).[4] Only Claire Maitland belongs to a medical drama, the other two are medically qualified professionals working as FBI agent and criminal pathologist, for law enforcement agencies. Nevertheless, the cover signalled a significant increase in the visibility of female medics during the 1990s either in lead or supporting roles, and in various kinds of medical genres. For example, there were Erica Matthews (Saskia Wickham) and Bev Glover (Amanda Burton) in the location-rich GP medical drama *Peak Practice*; Joanna Stevens (Amanda Redman) in a similar 'outback' GP drama, *Dangerfield* (BBC, 1990–99); Eleanor Bramwell (Jemma Redgrave) in the historicist medical drama *Bramwell* (ITV, 1998–); and Michaela Quinn (Jane Seymour) in another costume history (again, strongly revisionist), *Dr Quinn: Medicine Woman*; alongside Claire Maitland in the hospital are Barbara 'Baz' Hayes (Julia Watson) and Lisa 'Duffy' Duffin (Cathy Shipton) in *Casualty* and Susan Lewis (Sherry Stringfield), Carol Hathaway (Julianna Margulies), and Kerry Weaver (Laura Innes), among others, in *ER*; *Chicago Hope* and *Gideon's Crossing* also had major female characters but in a male-dominated ensemble cast.

The increasing visibility of women in these roles is in part a reflection of changes in recruitment in the outside world. In the UK between 1980 and 1993 the number of women working as GPs or in hospitals doubled. Women accounted for 25 per cent of UK doctors in the 1960s and by the 90s this had risen to around 50 per cent. Nevertheless there was also evidence of disproportional disillusionment among women working in healthcare. The major causes of disillusionment were reported as inflexible career structure, poor careers advice, 'lack of personal support systems and networks in medicine', poor working conditions, 'professional isolation' and a 'hostile, intrusive and aggressive' management culture.[5]

The increased entry of women into the workforce and their dissatisfaction with it was reflected in many drama genres and across the range of television programmes generally. The particular compromises that female television characters have to achieve, notably the balancing of career with the past aspirations of traditional femininity, are given a unique twist in the medical drama, since care and to some extent, nurturing, are as much professional duties as they may be desired goals of the personal sphere. Most of the characters mentioned in the list above are young or young-ish women without family or long-term romantic ties, and are prone to moments of doubt and introspection about the possibility of achieving either while maintaining their careers.

However, the critique of macho culture in healthcare, as it is articulated in the dramas, has the effect of producing men who are much more introspective, sensitive, and altogether less certain of their position in the world. This feminisation of male characters has the consequence that they are less sure of their position in the world of work, although this at least provides them with the opportunity to indulge in introspection, soul-searching and some retrogressive male bonding. For women doctors and nurses who occupy a similarly unanchored and potentially melancholic position, the rewards are harder to come by. I want to explore two female characters in order to flesh out the dramatic consequences of this inequality.

'Heartless bitches like me': Claire Maitland in *Cardiac Arrest*

Helen Baxendale's performance as the brilliant but mordant junior doctor Claire Maitland in *Cardiac Arrest* secured her place, for a time, as one of the strongest

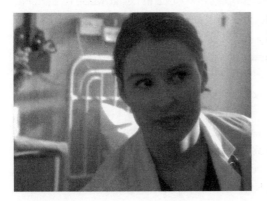

Cardiac Arrest's Claire Maitland (Helen Baxendale)

young female characters on television. She is the cool, competent 'hard-bitch' that coheres the series and provides a satisfying contrast to the anodyne co-star Andrew Collin (Andrew Lancel, see below). In particular it was her ability to participate in and ridicule the emergent 'lad culture' (reified most commonly through excessive drinking, intimate knowledge of football and the minutiae of trash culture) of her male colleagues while commanding an authoritative and often controlling presence over them. The mens' magazine *Esquire* positioned a photo of Baxendale under the headline, 'Doctor Froster: Icy TV medic brings a chill', with the commentary

> It is her ability to reduce us from Pearces to Southgates that make Helen
> Baxendale such a rare TV creature: a woman in control. And the dark eyes, pale
> skin and sensual curves that she reveals on screen makes us only too happy that she
> is in charge.[6]

This embrace of emasculation is nicely reinforced by the references to recent events in English football at the time – Stuart Pearce and Gareth Southgate had both missed decider penalties while playing for the national side (so the 'reduction' is from one kind of loser to a less 'macho' one) – while her positioning as object of desire is underpinned by the description of her face and body as akin to a figurine ('dark eyes, pale skin, sensual curves'). While the reference to nursery rhymes is appropriate given the infantile rhetoric, the commentary reveals what was an important aspect of her character's appeal: her apparent cold distance from cases of extreme trauma and her darkly comic cynicism.

Claire's persona was anticipated in series eight of *Casualty* with the character of junior doctor, Karen Goodliffe (Suzanna Hamilton) who is strikingly similar in terms of attitude, age and physique. Although competent as a physician, Karen is shown to be brusque and dismissive with other members of staff, rebellious in relation to hospital rules and inappropriately comic in her attitude to patients. In the episode 'Cat in Hell', she jokes to a man who has just had his hand severed in a train crash, 'It'll get you out of the washing up for a while'; but in contrast to *Cardiac Arrest* the programme aligns itself with the patient's response ('You stupid bitch, do you think it's funny?') and quickly contrives a situation where she is 'softened', using the death of a black boy as a means to provoke her tears.

Of all the female characters in *Cardiac Arrest* Claire most strongly reflects the influence of feminist discourses, but this is shown in the way that she absolutely rejects them while more peripheral characters (such as head nurse Julie Novac) continue to articulate their complaints in the terms of equal opportunities and discrimination. Claire is at least as hostile to female medical staff as she is to the men, in fact it is clear that she is more at home in male company that with women. Unlike the post-feminist figures discussed by Brunsdon we do not see her shop, dress-up, or struggle with the acquisition of appropriate cultural and social skills.[7] But she also remains conscious of the ideal femininity that has no prospect of being realised in the present world.

The adjacent figures in British drama of the mid-1990s are Anna Forbes (Daniela Nardini) in *This Life* (BBC, 1996–7) and Jane Penhaligon in *Cracker* (ITV, 1993–6). All three women work in traditionally male-dominated professions – medicine, law, police – but although they have clearly internalised and can articulate relevant feminist discourses, achieving equality *per se* is not the issue for any of them. Indeed, when such matters do occur they are largely tangential to both character and narrative. All are *initially* keenly ambitious and dedicated to their chosen profession, but as their series develop this is compromised by a fatalistic and cynical recognition that – despite feminism, and the advantages of youth – men continue to hold ultimate, and sometimes corrupt, power. Generically these characters are early manifestations of post-'equal opportunities' discourse, a group of television characters described by one of my (female) students as 'miserable bitches'.

But it would be a mistake to think that these characters experience *patriarchy* alone as oppressive, since they are as likely to be dissatisfied with the weak and flawed men in their lives as with the ones who actively frustrate their ambitions. Their fatalism is born of a feeling that the rewards offered by the world are poor ones, and yet they are unable to live up to its demands. Hence they do not entertain fantasies of 'having it all' – family, career, man – since the immediate instances of each are hardly desirable.[8] Claire's relationship with the married surgeon Adrian DeVries (Jack Fortune) is ultimately founded on little more than casual desire and he epitomises everything that is wrong with the NHS. Anna's desire for the (mostly) unavailable Miles (Jack Davenport) is a symptom of her aptitude for self-destruction. Indeed, this is a trait shared by all three so that in a distinctly non-feminist way each woman engineers her own downfall (Anna snorts cocaine in the company toilets and nearly loses her job, Penhaligon ambushes a colleague – who raped her – at gunpoint, and Claire reports to work drunk).

It is significant that all these women, at various times, are shown to smoke cigarettes (incessantly in Anna's case): Victor Perkins, referring to the smoking in *Letter from an Unknown Woman* (Ophuls, 1949) notes that, 'Cigarettes recur through the film as emblems of enslavement and unfulfilled appetite.'[9] While it is unwise to close the meaning of smoking for Anna, Jane and Claire as variations on those themes alone, there is a further sense of smoking, one that would not be relevant to a movie made in the 1940s: that smoking can be taken as a visible announcement of a loss of faith in one's own future, a commitment to slow suicide. In an era of persistent warnings of the potentially fatal health risks of smoking the message they are sending about themselves is clear.[10]

These characters and many of their colleagues are part of what I would characterise as the 'under thirty, no future' sensibility that is not gender- but generational-specific, that seemed prevalent in mid-1990s UK television drama. These are young professionals in well-paid jobs that have clearly defined career paths, and a good level of job security; despite this – perhaps because of its sense of predestined fate – their future seems bleak and uninteresting to them. It is important that male characters feel this sensibility as well, and all, in various ways, articulate the anxiety that they will become like their – often very unsatisfactory – parents. For the female characters in this situation the tension between the desire to compete on equal terms and the anticipation that the rewards of success will be unsatisfactory is keenly felt. There may be particular national reasons for the feelings embodied by these characters, since it is difficult to find similarly downbeat equivalents in US dramas.[11] Whatever the source of the feeling it is clear that, in Claire's case, her low expectations for herself and her career contribute to overall bleakness of *Cardiac Arrest*.

This is not to say that traditional conversations about equal opportunities and the difficulties faced by women in the medical profession are absent, but that they are made to serve a different, less instructional purpose. In 'The Glass Ceiling', Claire routinely criticises the struggling and obnoxious young medical student, Liz Reid (Caroline Trowbridge).[12] The equal opportunities discourse is confronted directly as a problem of training, when the single female consultant, Sarah Hudson (Selina Cadell), admonishes Claire for her treatment of Liz. Liz represents the next generation of house officers: a particularly uncaring figure who refuses to wear her glasses when on call (which leads to a lavage tube being knotted in a girl's stomach) and is favoured by the monstrous Graham Turner (as something of a daddy's girl); patients irritate her, she is not competent and shows little desire to learn. During a CPR we find that she does not know the basics of a procedure that would be familiar to television viewers (she forgets atropine and adrenaline). She is treated with barely disguised contempt by the others, so much so that when a nurse observes that 'Liz really does look dead beat', Andrew dismisses this as an act – 'She's been putting this on ever since she's worked here.' When Claire notices Liz sobbing she barks, 'Save the waterworks – it may fool the others but it doesn't cut any ice with me.'

Later, when Liz asks her for advice about a diabetic patient's blood sugar levels, Claire replies, 'I've told you what I think. Please yourself what you do.' When it is revealed that the patient's blood sugar is erratic, Sarah Hudson the consultant – who is businesslike but with a cautiously maternal manner, and the spokeswoman for a generation with a different access to the equal opportunities discourse – rebukes Claire for her failure to train Liz, in a classic senior-junior exchange:

Hudson: I accept that there's no love lost between you and Liz, what I cannot accept is when it affects patient care.

Claire: That's not my fault.

Hudson: It is your fault if Liz is scared to ask your advice in case you bite her head off. It is your fault that when I asked you to accept responsibility for teaching her you do so in a needlessly adversarial manner.

Claire: I believe in education through humiliation.

Hudson: Don't be flippant. Do you not realise we work under a glass ceiling? A female consultant, a female registrar, a female house officer – Graham Turner and his old boy network cronies would cream their pin-stripe suits if they knew what was going on – stop being such a bitch.

Claire: I'm sorry if I've let you down Dr Hudson.

Hudson: Claire, if you want to get where I have there is that ceiling to break through. There are plenty of people waiting to find fault, stop making it so bloody easy for them.

This dressing down has little impact on Claire and it does not change her attitude to Liz. Shortly after this exchange, we see Claire co-opted into a game of five-a-side football with the male junior doctors and joining in with their subsequent drinking in the recreation room. The lads praise her for being a good goalkeeper ('That's what comes from growing up with two brothers') but her cool performance is put off course when Cyril 'Scissors' Smedley (Peter O'Brien), who had a brief affair with Claire in the second season, admits that he is dating the head nurse Julie Novac. Claire is stunned and quickly offers to buy more drinks. Competition in the form of romance rather than career is shown to have the greater impact on her.

Claire demonstrates excellent medical skills but is brusque and sometimes brutally honest in her dealings with patients. Hence her 'badness' is not about a commitment to private healthcare, or about class and educational privilege, but is derived from her articulation of deep cynicism about the NHS, her life and the world. In *Cardiac Arrest* this is not necessarily 'bad' anyway, just true. Part of the show's appeal is the way in which an unfair, mean and often brutal environment is the fitting subject of her nasty black humour.

For example, the first episode of the third and final series, 'The Body Electric', begins with the iteration of generic action cliché, an ambulance trolley bursting through doors of casualty.[13] The young male trauma has suffered a brain haemorrhage during sex with his wife, to which Claire quips, 'One minute he was shagging, the next he's shagged'. Soon after when the prospects for recovery are gloomy, another doctor observes that 'He won't live', and Claire responds 'Who does?' thus announcing a central theme of this character (and this series): finding a life worthy of living (and of saving).

Her cruel flippancy does not last, however. Since the young man is brain-dead, this makes him a candidate for organ donation. One of Claire's patients is David (Frank Lauder) a long-term sufferer from a kidney disease and who regularly receives dialysis at the hospital. His treatment is reaching the end of the line however, and without a transplant he will die. To a certain extent David is used to 'soften' Claire in the third season of *Cardiac Arrest*, providing her with an outlet for the display of more compassionate care. Unlike the other patients he is shown to be cynical and knowledgeable about his disease; he has his own room furnished with cable television and at one point we see him playing chess with Claire. He calls her a 'slapper' and she says, affectionately for her, 'I always get the wankers'. Also, Claire's sympathy for his plight is shown putting her in direct conflict with the families of potential organ donors. Her attempts to convince them to allow transplantation mean that she has to verbalise her care (for him, for anyone). Throughout the third series there are several occasions where we are shown patients who are being kept alive artificially raising the question for their families and the medical staff about whether to 'the turn the machine off'. Because Claire's relationship with David is personal, her soliciting of patients' organs is directly unethical. While her decision to ask the parent of a recently dead boy for his organs is directly against the rules, breaking them is synonymous with the aspiration for personal development: 'For once in my life I'll do something right.' In a campaigning moment she admits her preference for a donor card opt-out, complaining that people don't carry donor cards 'so heartless bitches like me' get the job of convincing them. The parent, however, refuses: 'I don't expect you to understand,' he says, 'maybe you've never loved anyone.' That may be true, but Claire's world has little worthy of love to offer her.

Susan Lewis (Sherry Stringfield) and ER

Sherry Stringfield left during the third season of *ER* (1996) and returned to the show in season eight (2001); her portrayal of Dr Susan Lewis made her a popular character, one who combined a friendly bedside manner with dedicated commitment to ER care. Like Baxendale, Stringfield was in her twenties when she started in the show but, unlike Claire, Susan did not exhibit a world-weary cynicism. However, she did have conflicts with authority figures (a cardiac

ER's Susan Lewis (Sherry Stringfield)

consultant in the first series, Kerry Weaver [Laura Innes] in the second) and with her friend and potential romantic partner, Dr Mark Greene (Anthony Edwards).

The working relationship between Susan and Mark had solid romantic potential, the more so as Mark's marriage disintegrated. ER delays any consummation while stoking the audience's wish to see at least some admission of mutual desire acknowledged between them. This wish is bolstered by the elegant way in which Edwards and Stringfield portray the solid, playful friendship of their characters – a relationship that provides an emotional baseline when they disagree.

Beyond Mark, the prospect of romantic relations with a man is not foregrounded and late in the first season Susan is given an emotional burden that has a presence throughout the second. Her sister Chloe turns up at the ER heavily pregnant, and Susan delivers the baby, 'little Suzie'; Chloe eventually abandons it to Susan's care and disappears. In some ways this is a convenient miraculous birth for Susan since we subsequently see her coping with the realities of being a single working 'parent', while sidestepping awkward issues about fatherhood and the consequences of sexual romance.

While it is unclear whether Susan had imagined herself as a mother, she adopts the parental role with genuine tenderness and affection. Indeed those shots that frame Susan, Mark and Suzie together seem to visualise the fantasy of the happy family that elsewhere is shown to be either disintegrating or an unattainable ideal.[14]

To a certain extent the 'maternal' aspects of her job – care and nurture – are extended beyond the requirements of the professional code, so that she must take care not only of Suzie, but her sister too who is an infantile drug-user and heavily dependent on Susan's generosity ('She's thirty-four years old and she can't even part her hair'). The storyline also permits extensive exploration of the difficulties of the job with its unpredictable hours and the work of a single parent. Susan's ability to do her job is often compromised by her struggles to find adequate day-care and babysitting services, and brings her into direct conflict with Kerry Weaver who comments that Susan is 'not very adept at keeping her personal relations out of her work'.[15]

In the second season Chloe returns, reformed and rehabilitated, to take Suzie away. Susan is devastated and turns to therapy and smoking. In the therapy sessions, as Susan pours out her feelings, we see framed in the window a Catholic church, in a juxtaposition of the modern and pre-modern confessional.[16] The rest of her day is dominated by infants – her first trauma in that episode is a baby and she stumbles in on a christening service at the church. At the end of the episode Mark and Susan discuss her feelings while standing near the wide Chicago river.[17] Later she explains that she had something – the baby – and now all she has is work, which is not enough, and in a subsequent episode she turns down a promotion to chief resident.[18]

Whereas Claire's strong moral position and hedonistic personal life often led to conflict in her professional work, *ER* positions Susan as someone who is concerned to maintain her contentment with her job and her colleagues before professional advancement. Nevertheless, she is also someone who is shown to lack confidence in what she does, particularly in the early episodes. In 'Happy New Year' Susan treats a man complaining of chest pains; she runs some tests and brings the chart to her superior, Dr Kayson (Sam Anderson), who tells her to discharge him.[19] When she informs the patient he is clearly annoyed with having to wait for so long only to be told to visit his own GP, and Susan is apologetic. Subsequently, in an echo of the Maitland–Hudson conversation (above), Dr Hicks (C.C.H. Pounder) takes Susan aside for a benign senior-junior:

> *Hicks:* When I was a resident I was always worried about getting people's approval – the attending, the patients. Maybe because I was a woman, a black woman. Life was a lot easier once I got over it. *Don't* let the patients get to you Dr Lewis. We treat them as soon as we can and there is no need to apologise for how long it takes – we're a busy hospital not a restaurant.

This is in marked contrast to the brutal dressing down she receives from Kayson when the chest pain patient 'bounces back' to the ER with a heart attack and subsequently dies. Both Hicks and, in *Cardiac Arrest*, Hudson, are rare examples of women in positions of high seniority who are clearly products of an earlier equal opportunities movement that allowed them to join the ranks of male-dominated authority. By the second season Susan's main adversary was Kerry Weaver (Laura Innes), the dominating, crutch-laden ER doctor who quickly imposes her administrative and organisational authority on the entire ER. Before moving on to a consideration of the men in hospital dramas, it is worth pausing briefly on Kerry.

Kerry Weaver (Laura Innes) sets the
cameraman straight in *ER*, 'Ambush'

Kerry is caught between her own strong desire for career advancement, brittle
interpersonal relations with staff, and a commitment to academic publishing.
In terms of romance we only get hints at first that signal unusual (for *ER*) tastes
such as Mlungusi, a very tall African beau, and the implication that she has
written a romantic novel about the ER staff. When she is given a romantic
involvement there is a necessary compromise with her job. A relationship with
Ellis West, an HMO executive, was seen to cloud her judgment, as was her later
fraught lesbian relationship with the resident psychiatrist. Weaver is an odd figure
since she combines some of the unpleasant aspects of administrative and
bureaucratic rationality, which are often seen as corrosive to good hospital care,
and yet she is also clearly a good, competent doctor. Perhaps it is not so much
that she is unsympathetic but that her senior position as head of the ER distances
her from regular romantic opportunities. It was also her function, among a cast
of characters both male and female who have been emasculated, to energise
the narrative space with her aggressive colonisation of power. According to
Nancy San Martín:

> Even before she becomes the vehicle through which *ER* tries to make room for
> homosex, Kerry is lesbian-coded in stereotypically derogatory ways. Manipulatively
> pursuing promotion after promotion in medical administration, Kerry epitomises
> the castrating bitch, a woman empowered with dangerous phallic symbols – the
> cane she uses to walk (and occasionally to defend herself) and the sternal saw she
> often brandishes in the ER much to the consternation of her (mostly male) surgical
> colleagues.[20]

Lads and *Cardiac Arrest*

If the new hospital dramas sought to further demystify the idea of the male
doctor as God-like and all-powerful in the face of injury and disease, they also
exhibited a suspicious view of confident masculinity. As new hospital dramas

acknowledged the impact of popular feminism so too did they incorporate the growing criticism of masculinity that was emerging in cultural studies, criminology and psychology during the 1990s where masculinity began to be understood as pathological in itself.

For example, in 1997 the British Health Education Authority published a report citing masculine culture as a cause of ill health. It claimed that men were more likely to become ill and die sooner because of their 'macho culture', and issued a pamphlet, *The Healthy Man's Action Pack*, which argued that: 'men are more likely to become ill because of worries such as finding a role in life, employment, having somewhere to live, violence and personal relationships.' The report goes on to suggest that men are also less open to talking about their problems and this in itself is unhealthy: 'men's thinking seems to be dominated by negative factors brought on by fear, isolation and apathy.' A twist to this assumption is that the male 'stiff upper lip' is likely to dissuade them from visiting the doctor: 'men's macho attitudes make them less likely than women to visit their doctor when they are sick. When they finally do, their treatment costs more.'[21] Attitude and culture are linked to ill health which is in turn linked to the financial burden of treatment. More than that, abhorrent masculinity was seen as a factor in criminal behaviour with the then Shadow Home Secretary arguing that 'Western societies face huge problems with a generation of permanent male adolescents.'[22]

In *Cardiac Arrest* the culture of the junior doctors and the old boys' network of senior consultants are the backdrop to the exploration of masculinity, in particular 'Laddism'. 'Laddism' was a lifestyle promoted by magazines such as *Loaded* and one that was nostalgic for a world where men were certain of their roles as much as it self-consciously sought to offend the manners of political correctness. To some extent Laddism is the camp performance of masculinity.[23] Part of *The Nation's Health* critique of NHS culture concerned the oppressive macho attitude of doctors who were interested in technical and scientific advance (and golf) rather than the lives of their patients; there is a generic legacy here from the British 'Doctor in the House' films and books and the cultural currency of medical students' excessive high jinks.

The lads in *Cardiac Arrest* – James Mortimer (Jo Dow), Raj Rajah (Ahsen Bhatti), Phil Kirkby (Andrew Clover) and 'Scissors' Smedley (Peter O'Brien) – are delineated in terms of generation. It is the junior doctors who dominate the recreation room which is littered with the signs of late 1990s Laddism: a pool table, copious amounts of lager, and Oasis playing on the jukebox. But they occupy this performance with some difficulty: Scissors seems too old (mid-30s) for these games, James is gay and Philip is a public school boy for whom the retreat into lad culture seems more a response to being abandoned by senior consultants after they framed him on a manslaughter case. The only character apparently working class enough to be 'a lad' is Andrew (Andrew Lancel) – he is never shown drinking in the bar and neither does he exhibit any symptoms of Laddism. Their 'adultesant' life is perhaps best exemplified when James tells Claire that they will play football later, 'Five a side – meeting in the social club after *Star Trek*'. Throughout the third series Raj is continually berated by Scissors, James and Philip for capitulating to the demands of his long-term 'bird', Nazreen (Nisha K. Nayar), who wants him to educate himself through trips to the opera, 'subtitled films' and the theatre (James comments: 'She's a feminist – the sort who'll suck your knob but won't do your ironing because *that's* degrading').[24] The desire to protect the homosocial group from feminine contamination is seems to be a product of their anxiety about their present and future roles, and a recognition that the rewards of a successful career may not be worth the trouble. In this respect, although differently articulated they are similar to the female figures I discussed previously.

There is some poignancy attached to their behaviour since the offensive banter is part of a performance built on a desire for instant stimulation, not as a hedonistic end in itself, but as a compensation for the pleasureless medical world which the junior doctors inhabit. We see Raj enjoying sex with Kirsty, a student nurse, while he recites some medical jargon as a method of delay: 'I used to think about football – too stimulating – now I think about medicine.' The joke is often on the lads themselves and they know it. If the benefits of Laddism involve a shared community, it is also an isolating, infantile one exemplified when Scissors's partner, Julie Novac, refuses to go to the bar 'to listen to puerile banter with your sad loser mates'.

This form of Laddism is in contrast with the representations of masculinity in the 1980s when films and TV shows like *Wall Street* (1987) and *Capital City* (1989) valorised the macho yuppie culture. That earlier costume – striped shirt, braces and big car – is adopted by Adrian DeVries (Jack Fortune), the consultant surgeon. It is DeVries who sleeps with junior doctors, owns a Jaguar, and is racist, homophobic and just plain nasty; unlike the junior staff, he occupies and exploits a real position of power and influence, and the juniors reject his company (for example, after DeVries is thrown out by his wife he seeks solace in the recreation room and his attempts to strike up a conversation with the lads are rebuffed). What is Laddism but the masculine values of the 1980s *without the ambition* where what is left is not greed, desire, competition but the performance of lad-culture?[25]

Occasionally there are opportunities for otherwise laddish men to exhibit their care. For example, Raj is presented with a baby who, as a result of being hit by her mother, is seriously brain damaged. The discovery is made close to the end of the episode where Raj is desperate to attend a five-a-side football match, but his discovery of abuse transforms his urgent desire to be one of the lads, and the episode finishes with him turning away from the match and walking into the distance with his thoughts.

The function of sick, abused or dying children often is extreme enough to pull otherwise uncaring doctors into the realm of emotive involvement. For example, consultant surgeon DeVries discovers that he has a son by an ex-girlfriend (Debs, a nurse), and he decides to try to establish a relationship with him (initially by taking him to a football match). In an attempt to win sympathy from Claire, who is increasingly disillusioned with their sex-only relationship, he tells her, 'I have a son'. In the penultimate episode his son is involved in a serious road accident. We are treated to an action scene with a twist: the urgent resuscitation has somewhat calm cruelty as we are made aware that the other medical staff do not know why DeVries continues his attempts to revive the child – why, that is, he has suddenly discovered excess care. We see DeVries open his son's chest with a rib-spreader and apply cardiac massage accompanied by shots of the puzzled looks of other staff implying both, Why is he bothering? and also, Why is *he* bothering? After all his attempts fail he announces 'I'd like to be alone with my son,' and he cries, and kisses his son's shattered skull. No longer interested in Claire, at the end we see DeVries screaming into his mobile phone to his wife: 'I want to come home!' before collapsing distraught in the corridor.

Because it is anchored to a twenty- and thirty-something generation, Laddism could also be seen as an avoidance of the responsibilities of adulthood, a failure to leave adolescence behind. Although Laddism is a peculiarly British phenomenon, *ER* similarly frames masculine problems as part of a failure to become an adult.

Doug Ross in *ER*

In the episode 'Happy New Year' we see Doug Ross (George Clooney) and Linda Farrell (Andrea Parker), a pharmaceutical rep, having a post-coital conversation about the value of marriage.[26] As Linda hurriedly dresses, Doug lies back in bed in an introspective mood. He tells her about a couple he saw in the ER that day who had been married forty years, and wonders if he could hope for a similar future. Linda says she's not ready for that yet, which is why she is sleeping with him, and that he doesn't want that future anyway:

Doug: Why don't I want it?
Linda: Because you're afraid, most men are afraid.
Doug: Of what?
Linda: Responsibility, ageing, death, diminished sexual capacity.

Indeed Doug's failure to commit to his relationship with Carol Hathaway (Julianna Margulies) is a cause of her attempted suicide in the pilot episode, and he regards her subsequent engagement to the staff orthopaedist, John Taglieri (Rick Dougovich) with a mixture of wistful envy and adolescent jealousy, ultimately provoking a violent showdown.

Clooney's character was a popular heartthrob in the series, although, of all the characters in *ER*, Doug is less interesting in terms of his character's depth and complexity (he's a compassionate but playful rebel). He is interesting in relation to the programme's pathologisation of masculinity. Set against the sensitive, caring and sexually inexperienced Mark Greene, Doug often plays the part of naughty frat boy to Mark's straight man.

Like many of the other characters in new hospital dramas Doug's major conflicts are with authority, but in his case these are more strongly coded as parental figures, either because they usually are parents – Doug is an ER paediatrician – or because his own conflict with his father who abused and abandoned his mother is a recurrent theme in the show. Unlike Susan who often needs her confidence boosted, Doug's self-belief, his certainty that he is doing 'right by the children' pushes him to break hospital rules and into acrimonious conflict with his superiors. Furthermore he is coded, like the lads in *Cardiac Arrest*, as a hedonist, but unlike them he has no community of fellow drinkers with which to sublimate his sorrows.

Earlier examples of the genre may well have placed Doug as the central character; instead, *ER* makes Mark Greene central (insofar as there are any central characters in an ensemble piece). Their differences reveal a shift in emphasis in the genre from the good-looking 'action doctor' to the sensitive, gawky-looking everyman: indeed the close-up shots of Mark deep in thought imply an interiority that similar shots of Doug don't quite achieve. Nevertheless, Doug does get to play action man in a very physical episode, 'Hell and High Water' that institutes his partial rehabilitation.[27] By the second series Doug's

'acrimonious conflict with his superiors': Doug Ross (George Clooney) in *ER*, 'The Secret Sharer'

conflicts with his superiors has become grounds for not renewing his contract; the situation worsens when Mark, who has been staying in Doug's flat, discovers him in bed with Carter's girlfriend, a trainee doctor, Harper Tracy (Christine Elise) – a clear breach of professional and personal ethics. As a result Mark is unable to defend Doug adequately at a senior meeting set up to decide whether to renew his contract, and he is told to find another job. The episode 'Hell and High Water' dramatises Doug's moment of rehabilitation through naked heroism and excessive physical action.

The episode begins with Doug in a waiting room in a paediatrics clinic that turns out to be idyllic ('Ninety grand a year and nobody dies') and as he offers the job to Doug, the senior paediatrician says, 'We believe in continuity and commitment. Want to join our family?' Each of those nouns poses problems for the Doug we know up to now – his failure to commit to Carol Hathaway, his uneven and erratic work, and his conflicts with his father. Later, as Doug prepares to drive to meet his latest girlfriend at the opera, he gets a flat tyre. It is raining hard and, slumped in gloom in the car, he decides to smoke a joint. Before he does so a young boy knocks at the car window and screams that his brother has become trapped in a storm drain which is filling up with rainwater. In an extended sequence that draws heavily on the codes of the action movie, Doug desperately tries to rescue the boy and when he does so in the nick of time, co-opts a TV news helicopter to take him to the ER. The news team film him as the young boy becomes dangerously ill with hypothermia, and this is broadcast live, allowing the astonished doctors in the ER to witness Doug's remarkable heroism. The entire episode relies on taking Doug outside the site of professional conflict into an action arena more appropriate to a disaster movie. His compromised masculinity is therefore restored by fate, which deals him the opportunity to display his physical and professional competences 'in the field'.

Ultimately Doug's conflicts with authority are presented as a product of his unresolved relationship with his father. In the fourth season, Doug's father is killed in a car accident in the Californian desert, and he and Mark drive down from Chicago to attend to his effects. That episode, 'Fathers and Sons', is an example of the genre 'on holiday' and begins with a long, wide shot of the empty desert, rather like a Western or a road movie.[28] 'Fathers and Sons' explicitly places the concerns of medical drama into the *mise en scène* of the road movie. That genre is concerned with journeys of discovery, usually self-discovery, and the episode uses this as a baseline in order to develop and deepen the relationship between Doug Ross and Mark Greene.

Clooney's performance balances Doug's inarticulate childlike gestures against his vocal assertion of authority. He acts not with his face so much as his head, cocking it, often downwards, in a gesture of refusal, anger and thought achieved

Doug Ross (George Clooney) remembers his father in *ER*, 'Fathers and Sons'

at the speed of the gesture itself. This kind of intensity was well suited to the confined spaces of the ER, but Clooney was also emerging as a lead man in Hollywood with the action movie *The Peacemaker* (*ER* director/producer Mimi Leder, 1997) recently released at the cinemas, and the 'blockbuster' *Batman and Robin* released earlier that summer. He had already starred in the Quentin Tarantino-scripted horror movie *From Dusk Till Dawn* (Rodriguez, 1996) part of which, like 'Fathers and Sons', was filmed at Barstow in the Mojave desert. (In fact that episode is far superior to any of the above movies.) The movie connection is referenced by the unusual way in which the title caption 'Fathers and Sons' does not fade out but is pushed to the side and off-screen right, in the manner of *Psycho*, *Goodfellas*, and *From Dusk Till Dawn*. To some extent the episode is challenging cinema – it addresses the issue of 'what is a movie?' by regularly articulating itself and its characters in relation to screens, film and stars.

The episode begins in the very small 'sub-compact' car that Mark has hired, so that the generic confinement of *ER* is set against the backdrop of the epic John Ford landscape. It also raises the issue of the size of things – screens? TV? film? – as a theme. Like a small child Mark asks, 'Are we there yet?' and like a father Doug responds with sarcastic irritation. Later, in the teaser, we discover that Doug's father, drunk while driving, smashed into a truck, killing his girlfriend and the truck driver (a father of six children). 'I should've killed him myself,' says Doug as he tends the flowers at the desolate roadside where the accident happened. 'What a place to die.'

The other way in which memory is inscribed into the episode is through the picking over of Doug's father's things that remain in his motel room, untouched since the accident. We see photographs of the family on the mirror in the room, and as Mark and Doug study them, they are reflected in the mirror. Later, Greene removes the mirror and uses the plain space behind as an *ad hoc* screen on which to project Doug's father's Super-8 movies, where we see Doug as a baby being held by his father. Doug is clearly moved by this and the power of

ER's Doug Ross (George Clooney)
with Mark Greene (Anthony
Edwards) in *ER*, 'Father and Sons'
(note the Super-8mm projector in the
background)

the sequence seems to rest on Doug's gradual realisation that he loved his father
enough to hate him when he left, and that his father's nurturing and display of
these memories is indicative of his attachment to Doug.

Later Mark visits his own parents nearby and again we see how uncomfortable
the domestic family community is, in contrast to that of the ER. Mark meets
his father in the garage, turning some wood and is greeted by, 'What are you
doing here,' as his elderly father, an ex-Navy officer, reaches for cigarette. Here
cigarettes seem to function in order to occupy the mouth and hands as a means
of avoiding their potential for intimate expression. Mark's distaste for his father's
habit and his inability to communicate with him is revealed further during an
awful family dinnertime, after which we see Mark smoking too. After Mark's
father leaves in a coughing fit, Mark is seen smoking on the front deck with his
mother, reflecting that 'My father doesn't love me.'

Problems with authority are therefore not confined to the workplace but are
evident in the disparity of opinion and the poverty of interpersonal relationships
within families, something that is hinted at when we see patients and their
families arguing or beating each other in the ER, but more fully developed here
as a means to articulate a deeper account of the central characters of *ER*. For
Mark and Doug there are no appropriate role models, no guides to adulthood
that are satisfactory and they are thrown back onto their own uncertainties.

Doug's immature instincts push his character towards the uncertainties and
pleasures of adolescence rather than the burden of responsibility that adulthood
should bring. And yet Doug's encounters with adults – parents – reveal them
to be consistently inadequate carers. He is caught in a situation where his
allegiance to children sets him against the authority and law of the adult world.
He finally leaves the ER when he deliberately overdoses a terminally ill boy,
breaching professional code and without the knowledge or consent of the
parents; one of his final gestures as he leaves the ER is to tear his identity tag
from his coat and throw it to the floor.[29]

For men in these dramas the choice is between constantly bucking against authority in an often infantile display of resistance or, like the lads, retreating from authority and ambition, into a fantasy world of hard drinking, sport and science fiction.

Andrew Collin and *Cardiac Arrest*

Andrew Collin (Andrew Lancel) began work as a junior doctor in the first episode of *Cardiac Arrest* and, as we have seen, his learning curve matches our own as the series unfolds. His Christianity provides the occasional opportunity to introduce ethical issues into the narrative. (For example, the episode where he refuses to give a Jehovah's Witness a blood transfusion against his wishes, prompting Claire to accuse him of 'playing God'. He replies, 'You don't understand because you don't believe in anything.') He is mostly competent except when his inexperience and heavy workload compromise his judgment and, unusually for a central character, he is not exceptional or charismatic. Even by the third season we merely see him transformed from a hesitant, unconfident house officer to a slightly less hesitant and unconfident registrar.

One indication that he is not as straight-laced as he seems is the affair he conducts with Caroline (Jayne MacKenzie), one of the nurses on his ward. But rather than revealing a latent, perhaps interesting, aspect of his character, the sordid affair confirms his moral weakness and vulnerability to the random opportunities that confined working life offers. Early in the third series Caroline discovers that she has been exposed to HIV and tells Andrew, who is mortified since this threatens exposing his wife to the affair. Doctors with HIV in hospital dramas provide the opportunity to explore physical, moral and ethical issues related to AIDS over several episodes or seasons. The potential long-term latent phase of HIV means that such characters can always be potential carriers once they discover that they have been exposed to risk of infection; the decision whether or not to take an HIV test, waiting for the results, and explaining to

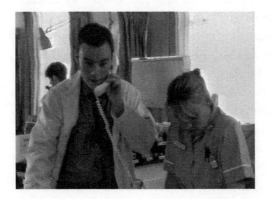

Cardiac Arrest, 'Death Us Do Part':
Dr Andrew Collin (Andrew Lancel)
gets a call from his wife; his mistress,
Nurse Caroline Richards (Jayne
MacKenzie) is next to him

seniors and partners, also provide the peaks and payoffs of many such narratives. The proximity to body fluids means an immediate danger of contagion of doctors by patients or patients by doctors, further disrupting doctor-patient and doctor-doctor relationships, as well as putting doctors at risk of suspension or redundancy.

Andrew is rarely the sole focus of *Cardiac Arrest*, except in one of the most distinctive episodes concentrated solely on his shift, and apparently shot in real time. 'The Red Queen' showcases the long-take steadicam style, with the first two shots lasting about five minutes.[30] This is interesting because the action and reflection modes are constituted within an overarching stylistic decision, with transitions between both modes happening in a single shot. The action develops in real time with Andrew, 'helped' by Liz Reid (Caroline Trowbridge), on ward duty, with that time also structured around Andrew's desire to visit the toilet which is continually frustrated by the demands of patients, his trainee and the combative hospital administration. The episode captures the gruelling nature of the job with adequate care attenuated by multiple and simultaneous demands on Andrew's attention. We see him hurriedly inform relatives of a patient's death as his bleeper goes off, while the hospital manager, Paul Tennant (Nick Palliser), criticises him for administering coronary treatment in a general ward; shortly after, senior consultant Graham Turner (Michael MacKenzie) arrives to criticise his telephone manner. The picture is of a doctor harried by management, patients and senior and junior staff while in the process of making some very serious medical decisions. In the middle of this he is phoned by his wife Alison and verbally harassed by Caroline.

The effect of this stylistic experiment is to present in relentless detail twenty-five minutes of the shift of a junior doctor. Although the harrowing events might have become wearisome to an audience, there is a somewhat fantastic change of tone towards the end of the episode. As Tennant follows Andrew like a shadow, dispensing criticism of his manner, treatment and attitude, he inevitably gets involved with cases as they present themselves. At one point a patient is brought in overdosed on heroin and collapses at their feet. On the soundtrack, an urgent trance/techno melody is played, as Andrew says, 'He's shutting down'. As he begins to administer treatment Tennant intervenes, worried about procedure: 'If he's on drugs shouldn't you wear gloves?' 'There's no time,' Andrew replies before Tennant himself helps Andrew with the treatment. Tennant is impressed by Andrew (and his own ability to help out) and Graham Turner arrives to congratulate Andrew on his fast thinking with another patient. Instead of glowing in the light of unexpected praise, Andrew just wants to shit. When he does reach the toilet a patient has collapsed inside, blocking the door. Tennant offers to take the door off its hinges and remove the patient, but then is forced to hold it up as Andrew goes in and we hear his relieved groans.

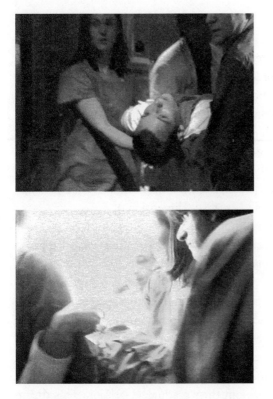

Cardiac Arrest, 'Death Us Do Part':
Dr Andrew Collin (Andrew Lancel) is
carried by his colleagues after being
stabbed by a patient...

... and is carried into the light

Like Mark Greene, Andrew represents the Everyman of the new hospital dramas, but unlike Mark even the potential for heroism has long since evaporated. Neither one of the lads, nor a Lothario, caught in an unhealthy affair, pressured by work, he is a character without character, but the series seems fascinated by his normality, his unexceptional status. In the final episode, it seems that Andrew himself is becoming weary of a world that is, at least in this series, the same day after gruelling day. He visits Liz Reid, who attempted to kill herself and is now confined in a room in the ward for the mentally disturbed. Shortly before, Caroline tells Andrew that she is pregnant, news that he finds at least as bad as when she told him of her HIV risk. He asks how Liz is, then offers: 'I had some news today ... I suppose we've all got our problems.' The therapeutic notion of sharing problems seems pointless and Andrew seems to recognise this, articulating his problems in a world that does not respond to such expectations. A little later he is stabbed by a psychopath (who has been posing as a doctor and executing patients in the ward) with a syringe-full of insulin. As he begins to lose consciousness, surrounded by his colleagues, his final diagnosis is centred on himself. 'Tell my wife ...' Images of Caroline announcing her pregnancy flash up, as Scissors prepares to cut the insulin from his stomach, and Andrew decides to leave the world without a final word for his wife or anybody else.

Romance

Medical dramas are famous for their romances: playing 'doctors and nurses' was always about exploring intimate relationships as much as it was about healing the sick. Managing the balance of love and work where both are realised in the same space provides a fertile basis for conflict and drama. In the early development of medical drama, many writers considered the 'soapy' melodramatic dimensions of such relationships to be a hindrance to the realist aspirations of their shows. But even where there was a resistance to soap storylines involving medical staff, the mere casting of attractive actors in the roles of doctors and nurses begged the question of what they did with their personal lives: workplace romance is, after all, a realistic dimension of life.

New hospital dramas tend to use the agony and disintegration of the body in two main ways: as a means to render a realist world in a hospital setting that confines its victims more or less malevolently to their fates; and as a means for the continuing characters to reflect upon their own interiority in such a world. The apocalyptic tone of many of the hospital dramas may seem at odds with the sensual and romantic satisfactions of a loving relationship: we might expect that fate and destiny may similarly condemn such relationships to decay and disintegration. It is a cliché that whereas classic Hollywood movies typically offer resolutions based around the formation of the couple, television begins with a happy couple and proceeds to work out their gradual separation. This truism needs to be modified since body trauma television may not even acknowledge long-term monogamous love as a realistic or desirable aspiration in the first place. Doug Ross spends most of the first and second seasons of *ER* refusing to accept what he sees as the constraints of commitment. In *Cardiac Arrest* Claire Maitland continually ridicules other characters that aspire to romantic satisfaction, a view that is endorsed in various ways by the programme itself. In *Chicago Hope* romantic love is a past ideal, like marriage, fondly remembered but pragmatically approached. Nevertheless, in a world where all human relationships are viewed with suspicion, the fantasy of romance persists, if in the face of the recognition that it is an impossible aspiration. The new hospital drama is constantly reminding itself of the pleasures and seductions of the old ones: the melodrama and romance of doctors and nurses. They are caught between the memory of 'the Dr Kildare/Mills & Boon romance of passion with disposable gloves, and the probes-and-pus business of real medicine'.[31] More than this, there is clearly little time left after work for romance: the pleasures of fast, immediate sensation – drinking, sex – are *all* that is left. Romance takes another kind of work, an imagination of another kind of future, and this is constantly complicated by the demands of work and its uncertainties.

We can link this to the changes in attitudes to work in the 1990s. Marriage is no longer a common destiny, and the expectation that men and women will work, marry and reproduce the values of society through their children is now severely circumscribed. What we see is a professionalisation of self-identity where the distinctions between work and home life, job and romance become a series of interlinked rule-bound choices. What makes *Cardiac Arrest* unremittingly bleak is the assertion that these choices are ultimately unrewarding, that the world is an unchanging place.

The potential for romantic relationships to affect the workplace has far-reaching ramifications in the hospital setting, with the possibility that bickering or full-scale conflict will jeopardise patient care as well as the division of medical labour. A typical senior-junior rebuke would be, 'Whatever your problems with [your colleague and lover] keep it away from your treatment of patients'. Staff who are no longer together and have suffered an acrimonious break-up provide a rich vein of conflict that may interfere with the delivery of effective healthcare. The residual potency of their shared romantic and sexual past insinuates itself into the new world where they are apart. As always, the problems this may cause have to be subordinated to the life and death stakes of trauma care, but they may also threaten its efficacy. When Peter Benton (Eriq LaSalle) and Jeanie Boulet (Gloria Reuben) break up their affair (she is married, but refuses to tell her husband as Peter requests) near the beginning of season two of *ER*, Jeanie is put on an ER rotation that means they have to work together. This provides an opportunity for Benton to express his anger, through his curt and sometimes downright nasty exploitation of his senior position, despite her requests that they should work together 'as professionals'. For a time, their personal conflict is displaced onto disagreements about medical care, but their exchanges carry the weight of what 'might have been'. While some temporary love interests may vanish from the show forever, this example tells us that the serial form allows us to experience what happens when 'happy ever after' is not the resolution, and former lovers have to work as a team in order to save lives.

The working out of romance in ensemble dramas is complicated and it is worth clarifying some of the possibilities and their problems. *ER*'s central romance for three seasons was figured between Doug Ross and Carol Hathaway; in keeping with its generic sophistication, the show starts with their separation and it is not until the final episode of season three that they kiss (with season four their relationship develops, albeit on rocky ground). The fact that this relationship is deferred, but its possibilities and problems are frequently hinted at, signals the remarkable resistance of the show to the simple rewards of a pairing up. Doug and Hathaway's prior, off-screen relationship – hinted at lasting two years – culminates in the latter's suicide attempt at the end of the pilot episode – hardly a secure foundation for reconciliation. Nevertheless, the aspirations to romance between them – as if aching for the rewards of traditional generic pleasures – are articulated intermittently, and separately. For example, there is their shared fond memory of workplace romance (before the series began) when they do a maintenance survey that takes them to the basement and a storage room.[32] Their prior involvement has a presence, a space in the hospital itself, and yet their reactions to it differ. For Hathaway that time was one of unhappiness, a time of self-loathing that culminated in her suicide attempt; for Doug, it was a period of uncomplicated sexual recreation. Their mutual recognition of the space, 'I didn't realise we were going down *this* hallway,' and the storage room which was the stage for their 'stolen moments', prompts Doug's bid for repetition: 'Should we?' However, Hathaway's startled, 'What?!' and his subsequent, 'Open the door?' delimits their differing relations to that time. Hathaway reflects that she has moved on and is now studying for her med school exams; Doug ruefully describes his regret at the loss of past happier times, before noting that his female psychiatrist wants him to talk about himself; instead he fobs her off with stories about his patients. As he explains his unhappiness he is lying on a mattress, with Hathaway on another sitting watching him, in a symbolic recreation of a therapeutic space. Romance is nostalgically located as a trace memory rather than an active possibility in the present; a memorable 'what if' is Susan Lewis and Mark Greene, but the show resists pairing them off as if it feared breaking them up again (which is what regularly happens with Carol and Doug when they do eventually get back together for a while).

The third series of *Cardiac Arrest* also confines the possibilities of romance to a distant past, in an old, less cynical world where such romances were possible. The elderly consultant Ernest Docherty (Tom Watson) and his new secretary, Isobel Trimble (Angela Douglas), find themselves attracted to one another, and much is made of the awkwardness of their courtship. Docherty procrastinates over asking her to marry him (she tells him to hurry up), and his desire to take her out dancing is frustrated by the demands of work (he is called to another hospital but cannot find transport to get back). Their romance was something only possible in the past; when Docherty announces his marriage in the bar Patsy Cline's version of 'Crazy' is playing on the jukebox. Their encounters in his office are rendered in a sepia yellow, accompanied by a mellow ambient electronic music, a kitsch simplicity, reminiscent of a chocolate box commercial from the 1970s. Docherty is a consultant urologist who reads 'International Bladder Update' (*Isobel*: 'Have you got your Bladder?') and the lighting, while connoting the pastness of old photographs, is also the colour of urine. The series ends with Docherty's wedding, and his mumbled speech to the young doctors present at the reception: 'I want to speak seriously to some of you young chaps ... if there is, er, if there is someone that you care about, er, you mustn't hesitate in letting them know.' This shoddy assertion of the value of romantic love, and the necessity of decisive action to secure one's partner seems of little use to the doctors in the new medical dramas.

Toxic patients and reflectors

Alongside management interference, one of the chief problems hospital staff encounter are their patients. The high turnover of patients in medical drama and the veritable zoo of medical oddities that are presented each week is of course a function of television's desire to maintain variety, diversity and novelty. Patients often present a set of physical and moral puzzles that the doctors need to solve, and are frequently a danger to themselves and others. Some fake their illnesses (Munchausen's syndrome) either to get attention, or to avoid some other responsibility; others are violent or abusive. Patients who refuse treatment are frequently depicted as suffering either mental disturbance or, in the case of male patients, from a macho refusal to be cared for. Indeed any potential criticism of the benefits of healthcare is closed down emphatically by depicting patients who refuse treatment as potentially crazy. Patients continue to present problems when they are unconscious or brain-dead. Issues of euthanasia and organ donation are often part of the new hospital drama narratives, bringing with them questions about the ownership of the body and its component parts. For example, in an episode of *Chicago Hope*'s first season a concert flautist has his finger bitten off by a mugger; the finger is recovered and reattached but it transpires that the mugger swallowed two fingers and the wrong one has been grafted on. This initiates a very strange legal debate between two patients, their lawyers and the medical staff about who owns the finger – the person it is sewn onto or the person who grew up with it.[33]

Rather than simply being environmental irritants or professional challenges, patients can also contribute to character development. This class of patient I call 'reflectors' because their situation broadly reflects that of the attending doctor, promoting recognition of a shared situation. 'Reflectors' implies the sense of return as to reflect means to cast back, 'to bend, turn or fold back; to give a backward bend or curve to (a thing)' (*Shorter OED*). Not only a mirror but also any surface, say a body or a human being, can cast back. For example, in *ER*, 'Of Past Regret and Future Fear', a chemical burn victim who is a fireman is brought into the ER; at first sight his condition seems superficial.[34] However, he has come into contact with deadly poison and Mark Greene has to inform him that it will eventually be fatal, with death occurring in twelve hours. Carol sits at his side as he reveals he has a wife and daughter who he is separated from, and that he has not seen his daughter in six years. This provokes Carol to think about her own life, and she reveals to him – and us – that her father killed himself when she was a child. *ER* frequently uses reflectors of this sort, where the main characters are often provoked into introspection or a change of mind by the actions, thoughts and feelings of their patients.

The following example from a recent *Casualty* demonstrates an alternative approach that privileges the stories of the patients as victims of abuse. 'No More Mr Nice Guy' is clearly influenced by the success of *ER* since, unlike episodes in previous seasons, it is far more mobile and fast paced with corridor shots rendered against a busy background.[35] We see a young girl, Louise Sutton (Juliet Cowan), with a badly sliced arm that she claims was caused by her mother. As the doctor treats her it becomes the premise for the discussion of the effects of her mother's alcoholism:

> She's an alcoholic. Till today I hadn't seen her since I was seven. She locked me in the flat and went on a two-week bender to get married to her new boyfriend. In Spain. She locked the door and told me to be quiet or the bogeyman would get me. *[Camera begins slow track in]* Ran out of food after the first week. Neighbour heard me crying, called the council. The police had to break the door down to get me out. They put me into care. It was in all the papers. I thought I must have done something wrong to make her lock me up like that. I only saw her once or twice after that, and that was in court. I spent the next nine years being pushed from pillar to post, children's home to foster home to children's home … mind you she did me a favour really. You know what they say, what doesn't kill you makes you stronger.

Later when her mother tries to comfort her, by offering to take her home, cook a meal get some shopping in, she brushes her away. Eventually the mother collapses and it transpires she has advanced jaundice as a result of cirrhosis of the liver: she is dying, but does not want to tell her daughter. The doctor informs the daughter and asks her to speak to her mother, who she has refused to see: 'It sounds to me like you need to say a few things to her, she is seriously ill and you may not get another chance.' Eventually they are reconciled much to the pleasure of the doctor; *Casualty* tends to foreground the therapeutic, counselling dimension of the medical staff's interactions with patients, so that the healing role is extended to the moral and interpersonal sphere.

While patients may be a toxic presence in the ward, doctors and hospitals themselves may cause more harm than whatever it is the patients came in for in the first place. For example, in an early episode of *Chicago Hope* Godfrey Nabitt (Jeremy Piven) was admitted with acute priapism after inhaling amyl nitrate. As the doctors treat him he develops several complications that nearly kill him. As Nabitt says after he recovers in bed from the first wave of complications,

> First you stick needles in my penis, then you gave me a heart attack with an injection, I get a computer put inside me, and now you want to cut out a clot because I've been lying down on my back too long? What kind of a hospital is this?

Eventually Nabitt sues the hospital, hiring a Jewish lawyer, Mr Wambaugh (Fyrush Finkel), who presents the hospital's catalogue of horrors to the assembled doctors:

> I was planning to save my bozo presentation for trial: that's where I'll talk about your chief of staff, who died in an MRI tunnel having sex with his assistant. I'll talk about the computer mix-up, which caused the Texas couple to bring their sick baby here for a heart transplant – only when they got here, you didn't have a heart. With [a Rabbi] you had a heart, but you dropped it on the floor, you kicked it around the room, and he died too. And today we're cutting off fingers that we attached to the wrong person … [my client] checked into this hospital with a simple condition but before he got out you cut into his heart, his leg, then his brain. I'm sure any jury will find your explanations completely acceptable because this is Chicago Hope.

Gideon's Crossing provides an example of the dire consequences of hospital care, using the familiar story of a basically healthy man being killed by medical treatment. The series foregrounds the wisdom of Ben Gideon (Andre Braugher) who is often seen lecturing to his assembled medical students. It is a good example of the way that the popular and critical success of *ER* made it the measure of all that came 'afterwards'. *Gideon's Crossing*, which premiered on the ABC network in October 2000, is clearly a new hospital drama, but it explicitly rejects *ER*'s distinguishing element – speed. 'If you look at a show like *ER*, every five minutes there'll be a gurney crashing through the doors' said Andre Braugher. 'This is a script that generated drama from an interior place.'

'The Mistake' begins with a woman trying to find out what has happened to her husband, David Porter, who came into the hospital with a minor condition.[36] It is revealed that he died of cardiac arrest and she is told, 'We used all of our capabilities but we were unable to save him.' This is followed by a wide shot of the lecture theatre – formalising the training aspect of the genre – where Gideon presents the case to his students and, over a series of flashbacks, we learn about the chain of mistakes that led to the man's unnecessary death.

The first doctor to treat him takes an EKG reading but when the results come back she is unsure if they are mixed up with another patient. Reluctant to ask for help, she takes a chance and administers treatment. After consulting with another junior doctor, they decide to explore his heart with a wire, and this causes a heart attack. Later, Porter suffers from a range of iatrogenic complaints including severe allergic reaction to the antibiotics he is given; he suffers kidney failure and eventually dies when, by sheer unlucky chance, a blood clot forms in the kidney dialysis machine. As Gideon subsequently says, 'A patient comes in healthy, we send him out dead. You know what that is? A clean kill. Might as well have taken the man into the street shot him in the head. Quicker, less painful.' The prospects of medical advance are therefore tempered by the realities of human mistakes and imperfections. As we shall see in the next chapter, the fact that doctors can be fallible is a rich source of drama for the new hospital dramas.

Notes

1. Although over the decade of *M*A*S*H* Nurse Houlihan developed 'from a comic authoritarian to a complex woman with a warm heart and a caring disposition toward the nurses she led as well as toward the doctors'.

2. A perversion that may not fully repress 'natural desires', as evidenced in the contrast between Hattie Jacques's grotesque Matron constraining the liberty of her nurses' and patients' desires while lusting after senior doctors, usually hapless and helpless figures played by Kenneth Williams. See *Carry on Doctor* (Gerald Thomas, 1968).

3. Charlotte Brunsdon, 'Structure of anxiety: recent British television crime fiction', *Screen*, vol. 39, no. 3 (Autumn 1998).

4. *Radio Times* (1–7 June 1996). Inside, Maitland is described as 'spectacularly unsympathetic' and the article (written by Alison Graham) comes to the conclusion that 'TV medical women are more deadpan than bedpan', p. 20.

5. Isobel Allen, 'What doctors want', in Jamie Harrison and Tim van Zwanenberg (eds), *GP Tomorrow* (Abingdon: Radcliffe Medical Press, 1998), p. 145.

6. *Esquire* (UK edition) (May 1997), p. 56. 'Working in a male-dominated world, she's got to be strong because female softness gets used', *Radio Times* (21–7 May 1994). Helen Baxendale's subsequent characters are considerably softened – in *Cold Feet* her character's chief desire is to get pregnant.

7. Charlotte Brunsdon, 'Post-feminism and shopping films', in *Screen Tastes* (London: Routledge, 1998).

8. Neither do they waste any time agonising over whether they are desirable – that is a given, or an irrelevance.

9. Victor Perkins, 'Same Tune Again', *CineAction* (Winter 2001).

10. There are also persistent campaigns to prevent the glamorisation of smoking on television;

we could say that these women use smoking as a badge of distinction and separation from official discourses.

11. Certainly the 1992–7 Conservative Government had the air of being dead on its feet, which may have contributed to this feeling of general gloom.

12. *Cardiac Arrest*, season 3, episode 7 (1996).

13. *Cardiac Arrest*, season 3, episode 1 (1996).

14. An example of this kind of shot occurs at the end of 'Motherhood' (season 1, episode 23, 1995), with Susan holding newly born Suzie near a window, and Carter jokingly pointing out the constellations. Carter was intermittently a romantic suitor for Susan, although she could not take his amorous advances seriously.

15. *ER*, 'Fire in the Belly', season 2, episode 19 (1996).

16. *ER*, 'Take These Broken Wings', season 2, episode 21 (1996).

17. The episode has other resonances of the mother-child separation theme, in particular a patient and mother, Loretta, a prostitute who Mark has befriended, is revealed to have terminal cancer.

18. *ER*, 'John Carter, MD', season 2, episode 22 (1996).

19. *ER*, 'Happy New Year', season 1, episode 11 (1995).

20. Nancy San Martín, 'Must See TV: Programming Identity on NBC Thursdays' in Mark Jancovich and James Lyons (eds), *Quality Popular Television* (London: BFI, 2003).

21. 'Men behaving badly pose a lethal risk to their health', *The Times* (10 June 1997), p. 10.

22. Jack Straw, review of the film *Kids* (1995) in *New Statesman and Society* (24 May 1996), p. 17.

23. 'Whereas in previous generations male machismo may have been a reflection of bullish self-confidence, Lad-ism, by contrast, is a faltering attempt to offset the unprecedented effects of what has become know as "the crisis of masculinity". While winking at the girls, it seems the Lads are really nodding at their own insecurities.' Andrew Calcutt, *White Noise: An A–Z of the Contradictions of Cyberculture* (Houndmills: Macmillan, 1999), p. 14.

24. *Cardiac Arrest*, 'The Glass Ceiling', season 3, episode 7 (1996).

25. To a certain extent the gallows humour and laddish performance began to dominate the third series of *Cardiac Arrest* which was initially 'hammocked' between two very popular examples of 'lads TV' – the sitcom *Men Behaving Badly* and *They Think It's All Over*, a comedy sports quiz with an aggressively male patois.

26. *ER*, 'Happy New Year', season 1, episode 11 (1995).

27. *ER*, 'Hell and High Water', season 2, episode 7 (1996).

28. *ER*, 'Fathers and Sons', season 4, episode 7 (1998).

29. *ER*, 'The Storm' season 5, episode 15 (1999).

30. *Cardiac Arrest*, 'The Red Queen', season 3, episode 4 (1996).

31. A. A. Gill, *The Sunday Times* (17 January 1999).

32. *ER*, 'Night Shift', season 3, episode 11 (1997).

33. *Chicago Hope*, 'Small Sacrifices', season 1, episode 13 (1994).
34. *ER*, 'Of Past Regret and Future Fear', season 4, episode 20 (1998).
35. *Casualty*, 'No More Mr Nice Guy', season 15, episode 9 (2001).
36. *Gideon's Crossing*, 'The Mistake', season 1, episode 5 (2000).

5

Playing God

Dr Greene: You cut across the lower segment of the uterus.
Dr Lewis: You're asking me?
Dr Greene: I'm asking God.[1]

The paradox that medical intervention may hasten death rather than prevent it has become a regular generic feature in new hospital dramas. Foregrounding of the moral and ethical issues that confront doctors means that the viewer is forced to confront an uncomfortable truth about their own mortality and the limits of medical care. Doctors kill people and this can be a 'good thing' in some episodes if it hastens the death of a terminal patient in great pain or quite the opposite if the killing is motivated by negligence, or worse, deliberate malice.

The latter extreme is rare and usually the stuff of horror movies, or thrillers. In *Paper Mask* Matthew (Paul McGann), who is posing as a doctor, kills a patient accidentally but also murders someone who threatened to uncover his true identity; in *Coma* (Crichton, 1978) a group of doctors arrange to send otherwise healthy patients into comas so that their bodies may be stored and used to harvest and sell their organs. Clearly, these are examples of doctors who are a great danger to the patients, acting in evil self-interest rather than loyalty to patients or professional codes.[2] Such figures are totally absent from the new hospital dramas but instead there is a large number who we do see as culpable for the deaths of their patients through mistakes or negligence or simply circumstance. In many instances only the audience is privy to a sense that the doctors may be culpable at all. So we can differentiate between those doctors who kill patients with deliberate malice (even if they suppose they are doing good) such as the real-life case of Dr Harold Shipman, the serial killer who killed his patients in his GP surgery, and those who are the victims of circumstance.

In new hospital dramas I want to consider the extent to which such cases foreground the doctors' increasing loss of confidence in their own ability to make decisions in these matters of life and death. We all know that doctors make life and death decisions as a matter of routine, but part of the hospital drama's ambition is to explore the dramatic potential of this fact. To a certain extent moral choices exist because of the limits on medical resources, and insofar as these limits are made part of the dramatic architecture of the genre they will be productive.

As I note earlier, the widespread distrust of the claims of medical science, public criticism of 'high-handed' doctors as gods of healing, and the contemporary absence of medical triumphalism have contributed to a lowering of expectations about the potential achievements of medical care. The fact that doctors cannot save everyone is frequently restated using the senior-junior address, to the effect that 'You can't play God', a remark that combines the accusation of unsubstantiated grandiosity with childish fantasy. Less a statement of rational fact, 'you can't play God' has become the mantra of the lowered expectations of doctors' abilities; 'playing God' is seen as an expression of unqualified arrogance and overconfidence, itself not conducive to being a good doctor. Very few of the doctors aspire to play God and when they try they are typically coded as a toxic presence in the medical community such as *ER*'s Robert 'Rocket' Romano (Paul McCrane).

There are gradations of what we might call 'toxic care' across all characters, ranging from Raj giving a begging cardiac patient one of his cigarettes in *Cardiac Arrest* which results in the combustion of the patient's oxygen tank that demolishes part of the ward,[3] to Mark Greene's deliberate, secret, refusal to administer defibrillation to a patient – who had gone on a shooting spree that morning, threatening Mark's own family – which results in the patient's death.[4] In that case Mark's 'murder weapon' is doing nothing, his refusal to provide medical treatment, and clearly he is in a position to play God either to save the man or let him die. I want to concentrate on two major examples from *ER* where playing God is both a freely chosen moral position and one forced on the doctor by circumstance and fate.

'Carter's Choice'
The *ER* fourth season episode, 'Carter's Choice', concludes a story arc established over several episodes where a number of elderly victims of a serial rapist are treated in the ER.[5] The first trauma occurs during the teaser when a security guard is brought in with terrible chest injuries; it is established that he saved another elderly woman from the rape. At the same time we hear that the ER blood supply is scarce due to a delay at the airport caused by a storm (an act of God?). In a particularly bloody action scene, Carter performs a thoracotomy, and transfuses more blood ('How much?' 'All of it!'), but Mark points out that the heart is 'shredded' and advises Carter to 'Call it. Save the blood.' Mark's pragmatism contrasts with Carter's judgment of his treatment as morally justified on the grounds that, 'He stopped an old woman from being

raped.' Mark's somewhat gloomy response – 'No good deed goes unpunished' – implies that his pragmatic judgment is linked to a fatalistic recognition of the oppressive and malevolent world that *ER* inhabits. Nevertheless Carter gives up soon after and asks for time of death; as Anna (Maria Bello) says '6.11', Carter violently slams his scalpel into a tray, and rips off his latex gloves in frustration as he exits the room, saying 'Bitch!'

The sequence foreshadows the moral complexity that the viewer will later be confronted with. The extreme nature of the guard's injuries coupled with his heroic actions encourage strong audience proximity to the efforts of the doctors in trying to save him; however, the fatal extent of those injuries and the shortage of blood, which could be used to treat cases with better prospects for survival, means that we are sympathetic to Mark's pragmatism. Furthermore, Carter's own 'heroic' efforts to save the doomed guard, itself a regular feature in the genre, seems motivated by personal commitment rather than medical professionalism (he has an elderly grandmother). Our alignment with Carter is further compromised by his anger at the guard's death which is expressed in an unusually violent manner: as he slams the scalpel down we get a quick shot of Anna flinching (as if she believed it was intended for her), followed by a longer shot of Carter leaving the room as she looks on in fear and astonishment. Indeed his choice of the word 'bitch' implies that masculine aggression provides the emotional energy for his behaviour, that in some way Carter's emotional frustration locates the 'bitch' in Anna herself as the one who officially called the time of death.

Later the elderly victim is wheeled in and, again, Carter, Greene and Anna begin treatment. As before, the extent of her injuries – she has been half-strangled and thrown down the stairs – encourages strong viewer proximity with the actions of the medical staff to heal her. That proximity is partially displaced from her to the doctors since, apart from her obvious physical status as an injured old woman, like the guard she is unconscious and we learn nothing more about her. As he examines her abdomen Carter discovers that the rapist has carved the word 'WHORE' into her skin with a knife, and reports this to Greene with a mixture of disgust and barely disguised anger. Although the woman is saved (and, in a later scene, Anna confirms that she was not raped), Carter expresses his disgust at the rapist, suggesting that someone should shoot him and 'toss him in the back of a dumpster'. Carter's violent desires for retribution, hinted at in the teaser, now find further assent when Mark announces to the staff that the rapist has been shot by the police and he is being brought in to the ER for emergency treatment. Most of Greene's colleagues object saying, 'we don't want him – send him to Mercy'.

As the rapist is brought into the ER it is clear that he has suffered serious injuries not unlike that of the guard. However, there is no corresponding action scene: Carter, Anna and the nurses seem paralysed at the prospect of treating him and their attitude and our knowledge of the outcome of his crimes encourage distance. When Mark, in teaching mode, asks, 'What do you want to do Dr Carter?' a nurse replies, 'Let the bastard die'. In order to recruit some action, Mark appeals to the professional code arguing that, 'He's a patient – like every other patient he gets our best effort'. However, as viewers we are caught between competing moral systems: for on the one hand, it is certainly the case that doctors should treat injured people effectively; on the other the young man has been framed as a violent rapist who has already killed a security guard and seriously injured an old woman. Our alignment with Mark as the moral centre of the show and Carter's history of conflating personal concerns with professional procedure may weigh against the latter. But the inaction of the nurses, transforming this generic action scene into virtual stasis, promotes the sense of general assent to withholding treatment, since all of them have been established (albeit briefly) as altruistic, generous individuals rather than executors. At this point Mark's professional pragmatism seems to come at the cost of moral sensitivity.

Soon after Mark is called away to another trauma case and Carter takes over treatment. As he is performing a chest drain a jet of blood drenches his gown and Anna tells Carter he has lost a litre of blood and needs a transfusion but Carter asks for 'auto-transfusion', a less reliable process that involves re-circulating the patient's own blood loss back into the body. Although the rapist survives, it is clear that Anna considers Carter to have broken a fundamental moral and professional code. Subsequently the moral ambiguity of the case is clarified in two reflection scenes between Carter and Anna:

Anna: Why didn't you use the blood on hand?

Carter: It's all we had.

Anna: So? We used six units on that guard this morning we were short then and you didn't even blink. Why not use the blood on the kid?

Carter: I thought auto-transfusion was the best course of action.

Anna: Oh *please*! We could have done a thoracotomy, we could have pumped in blood on the rapid infuser.

Carter: Yeah, well, he lived, he's in recovery.

Anna: Dumb luck. You are one of the most aggressive physicians I have ever seen in trauma and you auto-transfuse him? You didn't want to waste the blood on the kid; you didn't care if he lived or died.

Carter: It's my trauma, it's my call.

Anna: Would you have done it differently if the patient hadn't been a rapist?

Carter: Every case is different.
Anna: Did you withhold treatment from that kid?
Carter: No.
Anna: John, did you withhold treatment?
Carter: [quietly] No.

The conversation moves from Carter's attempts to secure justification of his actions to a defensive refusal to acknowledge that his moral decision can be framed as a breach of professional ethics. Nevertheless, Carter's quiet 'No' at the end signals the crumbling of the already shaky foundations of his moral rectitude. This is made explicit in a scene at the very end when Anna discovers Carter waiting for her in the dark on the stairs outside her apartment. He is holding a bottle of whiskey, a visual admission at least that his actions have provoked an uncomfortable emotional pressure that needs to be suppressed. As we have seen his earlier assertion of violent masculinity has the effect of distancing us from his decision, particularly the use of the word 'bitch' which belongs to the same, if more extremely articulated, class of misogyny as the rapist's use of 'whore'. But here, Carter has abandoned this apparently assertive gait and withdrawn to a huddled figure crouching on the stairs. His speech to Anna – performed in a manner that underlines his uncertainty – has the effect of clarifying the ambiguous nature of these events for the viewer as well as emphasising Carter's gradual shift from a moral calculus that counter-factually justifies his actions to a deeper realisation of his existential responsibility for what he did (or didn't) do:

I wanted him to die. I saw what he did to that old lady. And the others before and I wanted him to die. I didn't think he should have that blood – I mean if somebody had come in and they really needed it – if some little kid had been hit by a car or some old guy had been accidentally shot … If someone like that had died because we wasted the blood on that guy … I don't know … It's my decision and I made it. And if he'd died I don't know how I'd feel. But I can't say that I'm sorry. I mean was I wrong – Anna are you sure?

Anna replies that she isn't sure either, in marked contrast to her earlier moral outrage, suggesting that her allegiance to the professional code is less secure that we might have thought. Mark, too, tells Doug Ross that 'we saved the rapist today – hell of a world, isn't it?' similarly implying that his professionalism is in tension with his larger sense of an absurd and unfair environment. Anna takes Carter's hand as he begins to weep and the episode ends as we hear a siren, an aural suggestion that such problems are not going to go away.

of the ER with the patient on a gurney and we get a speedy steadicam shot, accompanied by fast drum music, that follows them down a busy corridor. Trainee doctor Chen fails to avoid them and spills her tray, foreshadowing her discomfort with the geography of the ER, which becomes important later. The subsequent action scene, shot in continuous steadicam – probably the *acme* of action scenes – serves to reassure the viewer, despite the horror of some injuries, since it shows the efficient division of medical labour as well as the expert choreography between performers and steadicam. The fast camera movement does not create disorientation but a sense of overloaded and expertly choreographed *mise en scène* as the camera takes in the main characters, as well as distant glimpses of peripheral detail. In addition to visual excess we get an aural assault on the senses, with monitoring machines beeping and alarming, alongside the fast-talking medical speech.

For example, as we see Benton attending to his mother Carter suggests that he gets a spine test and Benton barks, 'Get the hell out of here'; Carter moves to trauma two with Susan Lewis through the swing doors that divide the two rooms, and the camera follows. Mark uses Carter's entrance as an opportunity for teaching and quizzes him (and Chen) on the next course of treatment; in a comic moment both of them get it wrong and the nurses supply the correct answers. Then we pick up the movement of a nurse into trauma one, the camera moving close to Mae in pain, then sweeping up over the heads of the nurse and Benton barking instructions.

At this point the continuous take is replaced by a rapidly cut sequence that serves to emphasise particular reactions. The nurse, Haleh (Yvette Freeman), tells Mae that they need to undress her, but Mae objects in tears and says, 'Please, not in front of Petey':

Haleh: Peter? Peter?
Benton: [absorbed in treatment] What?!
Haleh: She doesn't want to be naked in front of her son.

We see his face soften as he realises she is not another patient but his mother; this softening is a vital element in his character arc, that shows him gradually abandoning his robot-like dedication to his career and learning to appreciate the feelings of patients and their families. Indeed, he seemed oblivious to the discomfort of his mother before this point, shouting 'Call the chief of orthopaedics and tell him to get off his ass now!' and he subsequently uses the fact that the patient is his mother as means to challenge the authority of the senior surgeon.

As Benton leaves his mother in the trauma room and swoops his hand over his hair in a gesture of frustration, another hospital nurse is walking quickly by which motivates another camera movement, leaving Benton and following the nurse back into trauma two. By now regular viewers are attuned to the way in which camera movement may be motivated by peripheral characters' movement, or indeed by nothing more than anticipation. It is worth saying that although the camera seems to follow discovered action it in no way replicates the visual style of documentary or vérité forms, because it reacts, moves and anticipates (often literally confined to small spaces) with the agility of any other staff member. The view we get of the ER seems less observational than embedded, like the characters and patients, in the action itself.

As we enter trauma two we hear Mark's ominous announcement, 'He's going down the tubes,' and we get an agile rendering of the details of medical treatment with Mark calm and authoritative while also conveying the urgency of the case. Again, Mark uses the patient's worsening condition pedagogically (and somewhat chirpily):

Mark: We gotta crack his chest … we do a thoracotomy when?
Chen: A penetrating trauma and full arrest?
Mark: Exactamundo!

As he does the procedure we see no insertion or cutting, but the eager observant faces of Chen and Carter leaning in to observe, while Mark gives a commentary, 'I'm in … pericardium's dry …' The patient is saved and Mark leaves the room with Susan.

In contrast with the rattled Benton, Mark is shown as unflappable and confident in his expert treatment of a serious trauma case, even to the extent that he is able to teach and work simultaneously.

This continues after the title sequence where the first patient we see Carter treating is a man covered in tattoos, Mr Longet, who at the request of his current partner attempted to remove the name of a former girlfriend on his bicep, using a power sander. This is the first in a number of comic patient cases (although as we shall see, there are serious undertones to it as well) with Mark using Longet as a teaching case for Carter, and suggesting that 'We'll have to do a graft – we could move that serpent head'. Longet objects, 'Onto the body of a goddess?!' and Mark and Carter leave smirking.

There then follows an extended reinforcement of Mark's confidence and commitment articulated through his generous treatment and advice to Carter. A continuous shot of them walking along various corridors (again, packed with glimpses of peripheral details, people, etc.) is a good example of mobile dialogue in the workplace. After Carter admits he hasn't eaten lunch, Mark miraculously produces a candy bar from his back pocket and borrows a pen from Carter, signalling the extent of his nurturing and care as well as mutual trust. When Carter congratulates Mark on getting the attending position, Mark seems more distant and uncomfortable and says it is not confirmed yet.

> *Carter:* A lifetime of this, huh?
> *Greene:* The ER it's great … you get skilled in *every* aspect of medicine, you see a *variety* of cases, you have an *immediate* effect upon your patients' lives, but mainly – it's like joining a circus.

At 'effect on your patients' lives' Carter's grin becomes a chuckle, no doubt in recognition of the slightly parodic nature of Mark's sell (confirmed when a bearded man in a gold lamé ballet dress passes as he says 'circus'), but perhaps also a hint that the 'effect' on patients is not necessarily benign. Mark's description neatly encompasses the attractions of *ER* itself, its elastic range and exaggerated performative appeal. It also signals Mark's playful enthusiasm for his job, which at this point we have no reason to doubt.

Soon after, Mark meets the O'Briens for the first time but their importance is cloaked by a variety of other patient cases and character vignettes, as well as Benton's story arc. We see Benton pacing back and forth in the waiting room outside the surgery with his sister Jackie and her children sitting nearby, until Benton tries to goad her into blaming him for the accident – 'It's my fault that this happened, right, I'm so pig-headed and self-centred, right?' To an extent Benton's self-criticism, fantasised as his sister's is quite accurate: exhausted from overwork he was asleep when Mae called him from the top of the stairs and her subsequent efforts to climb down resulted in her falling. Like Mark, Benton's obligation to his family is subordinate to the job but as we have seen with Mark there is an emotional price to be paid for this that ultimately affects working life as well.

It is important that we see Jodi and Sean O'Brien before Mark does, albeit briefly, because it establishes their intimacy with one another rather than tying our introduction to them as part of Mark's doing the rounds. They are waiting in an examination room, the heavily pregnant Jodi walking rather stiffly and slowly and Sean very close behind attempting to tie her gown. They are both laughing, and when Jodi says, 'I'm as big as a house', Sean nuzzles his head in her neck for an intimate kiss. They are immediately interrupted by Mark's sudden entry and jump back embarrassed, as if caught out. Mark is civil and businesslike, examining Jodi and offering the diagnosis that she has a simple bladder infection. During this scene Jodi's dialogue and the framing of Sean and Jodi together emphasise their open physicality with one another and in particular

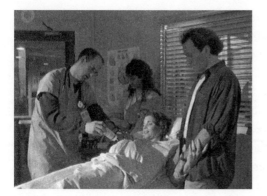

Expectant couple: Jodi and Sean O'Brien (Colleen Flynn and Bradley Whitford) are seen by Mark Greene (Anthony Edwards) in *ER*, 'Love's Labor Lost'

the cheerful ease and humour with which Jodi discusses her body. When Mark begins his examination of Jodi on the bed Sean is holding his wife's hand and gently caressing her arm; a couple of shots later we see Jodi caressing her husband's arm as well with her ring hand, so that idealisation of the model, modern, married expectant couple is complete.

Mark's slightly awkward response – which I sense as partly what he *doesn't* say or do – can be taken in two ways: either he does not notice their cheery happiness, since the case is so routine it is boring for him, or the unusual sight of a happy couple (given that most couples in the ER are over-anxious or bickering or worse) has disarmed him, especially since his own relationship is in trouble.

At this point in the episode the O'Briens can be seen as another case in the line of mildly comic and mostly genial patients we have seen up to now. A few scenes later Mark returns to the O'Briens with Chen and Carter and this time we follow them into the room, where Mark asks the students what they think of Jodi's test results. Chen obediently says to Mark, 'Simple cystitis. Fluids, rest and a course of Bactrim' – which is the textbook answer although Carter, ever sensitive to the feelings of the patients and looking for one-upmanship, turns to Jodi and Sean to translate: 'It's a bladder infection.' Mark continues to instruct them as they leave the room and encounter Doug Ross in the corridor who quips, 'He saves lives, he teaches, he slices and dices' – another prophetic comment, since Mark will end up slicing flesh soon. A few scenes later we pick up Chen complaining to Carter that 'everyone is so old and sick around here' ('Yeah, this is a hospital') but her words are proven wrong when Sean bursts in and says that Jodi is unconscious in the car.

As she is wheeled into the treatment room a caption signals the time at 7.15 pm, roughly a full shift after we first saw Mark playing football outside. In contrast to the easy physicality and stiffness of our earlier encounter with them the O'Briens now seem like a much more typical ER couple – highly anxious and distressed. Jodi is having seizures and, in the first extended action scene since the teaser, we see the medical staff struggling to restrain her bucking body, as alarms whine and beep loudly. The steadicam circling the table glimpses her flickering eyelids, the nurses holding down her legs, and the attempt to put a finger across Jodi's teeth to prevent her biting her tongue. This is the unruly body that compromises medical attention, a real fight to make her well. At one point Mark tries to put a large needle in her external jugular but her shaking body makes this delicate procedure highly dangerous, although Mark is clear-headed enough at this point to do it successfully and Jodi is stabilised.

At this point, Mark can still command authority and is apparently unshaken by Jodi's surprising change of fortune. After checking the foetus's heartbeat and doing an internal examination on Jodi, Mark switches to reflection mode and explains what has happened to Sean:

> *Sean:* Doctor what the hell's going on?
> *Mark:* Your wife has a condition of late pregnancy known as eclampsia: the blood
> vessels go into spasm causing a lack of oxygen to the brain, which leads to seizures.

However, when Susan arrives to start her shift we are reminded by her return that Mark's is technically over, a warning that exhaustion can be dangerous (as we saw with Benton). Susan hears Mark's account of Jodi and offers to take over, but he refuses citing his responsibility as the doctor who gave the mistaken diagnosis:

> *Mark:* … it's not about you, it's me, I saw her earlier and I diagnosed UTI, sent her
> out and she seized in the parking lot.
> *Susan:* Oops.
> *Mark:* Yeah, I thought the protein in her urine was due to cystitis and I blew off
> one borderline BP. I'd feel better if I saw her through.

His personal reasons are connected with his sense of damaged self-worth and possible incompetence, demonstrated in the conspiratorial manner in which he checks around the corridor before confessing his mistake to Susan. It is also at this point that it becomes clearer that this story will dominate the rest of the episode as we see less and less of other cases (such as Benton and his mother).

Later we see Mark on the telephone to the OB department, saying, 'I feel very comfortable, I've delivered a couple of babies.' We learn that the OB attending, Janet Coburn (Amy Aquino), is away at another hospital and won't be back for a while, while the young OB resident on call, Drake (Bradford Drazen), is called away by his bleeper. Clearly, the implication that Mark may not be 'comfortable' in delivering the O'Brien baby rattles him as if questions about his competence are not confined to his own sense of responsibility. This is evident in his sarcastic manner with Drake where again the issue of his competence is verbalised:

> *Drake:* Do you feel competent to handle this down here without me, we're getting slammed upstairs [in the OB].
> *Mark:* Yeah, I think I can muddle through.
> *Drake:* I'll check back with you at say, 23 hundred?
> *Mark:* Roger.

With Jodi now awake and back (almost) to her normal cheery self, we see the couple discussing names as Mark performs an ultrasound, teaching Carter in the process, his authority and calm apparently restored. When they ask Mark to decide on a name, he says, 'Jared is on both lists – compromise is the soul of marriage. Jared it is' – a comment tinged, unconsciously of course, with irony. Jodi is now having frequent contractions and Mark conducts a vaginal examination, while Carter peers over his shoulder eagerly. Although there is never any suggestion of prurience, it is an odd picture – shot from the approximate position of Jodi's head – since Carter's enthusiasm is both serious and also comic:

> *Jodi: [to Carter]* Do you wanna look too?
> *Carter:* May I?
> *Jodi:* Why not? – everyone else has been poking around in there.

Later Mark inserts a scalp monitor to the baby's head, and Jodi again remarks on the comic nature of Carter's interest in her vagina:

> *Jodi:* Enjoying the show?
> *Carter: [fascinated]* Yeah *[looks up, sheepish]* I mean, no.

This elicits a wry smile from Sean, who continues to stroke her hair, but the exchange also signals the continuing and contradictory importance of her vagina. Jodi's question raises the possibility of improper pleasure derived from her 'display' as Carter's reaction acknowledges. In fact, far from an object of fascination, her vagina becomes part of subsequent problems.

Near to midnight the baby's heartbeat drops and Jodi begins the final stages of labour. At first this seems like a classic birth scene, with Jodi crying out in agony and aggressively brushing aside her husband's attempts to coach her breathing technique. In fact we might wish to read this as another comic moment, since it reverses their earlier harmonious relationship. Nevertheless the scene is tinged with ominous signs that Mark is not confident about the outcome, and he asks Carol in a whispered aside, for an ETA on Coburn's arrival.

When Susan announces another problem result from the monitors, Mark responds with treatment and asks Carol to contact OB and page Coburn again; Susan turns to look at him, but he does not meet her gaze. When Sean asks if there is anything wrong, Mark replies, 'No, we're OK,' but Susan's concerned glance at him implies that all is not well.

The next caption announces the time at 3.15am and we see Mark on the phone begging OB to take Jodi because 'she's inches away and the epidural's wearing off'. After raising the possibility that Jodi may soon be in even greater pain we see her screaming in agony as Mark tells her to start pushing. Sean counts alongside her as we get a harrowing series of shots with the medical staff shouting at her to push, while Sean – somewhat redundantly – repeatedly counts up to ten. This medley of shots ends with Jodi screaming, 'I can't! I can't get it out!'

At this point Mark is ready to voice his uncertainty in public, telling Carter to 'drag Drake [the young OB resident] down' and telling Susan that 'She's not progressing, the baby's heartbeat is dangerously low, I'm gonna start the pudendal block.' Chen is watching this exchange and her shocked expression is visible when Mark prepares a very long needle, squirting a small amount of anaesthetic from its end. Ordinarily this would be a purely comic shot – the patient overwhelmed by the size of a needle that will be stabbed into them, but here it is another doctor, albeit a junior, who is struck in anticipation of the visceral impact of the needle. Indeed, from here on both juniors, Carter and Chen, are less students than surrogates for the audience variously horrified, terrified and distressed by the horrific events they witness.

Another caption takes us to an hour later with Carter running down the stairs and into the treatment room before telling Mark that OB is 'busy with two c-sections'; leaving this movement the camera picks up Mark and Susan. Mark is now clearly losing control in the face of an obstructive and unresponsive pregnant body:

Susan: Mark, Mark, no one will blame you if you wait for OB.

Mark: The baby monitor says now or never.

Susan: Why put your ass on the line?

Mark: Because I've come this far and I'm gonna see it through.

Mark's personal commitment to the treatment may have significant conse-

quences for his career (his promotion), and the fact that OB has already
challenged his competency means he has something to prove. It is not just that
the baby monitor is telling him to carry on, it is a question of his own integrity
as a doctor.

What follows is the first sustained assault on the viewer's senses and it will
continue virtually without rest for the remainder of the episode. All other
narrative and character strands disappear. As Mark clanks the forceps in a tray
of antiseptic, he tells Susan to 'cut a medium episiotomy' (an incision that widens
the opening of the vagina). Jodi's vagina is no longer the object of the fascinated
diagnostic gaze, but an obstruction that needs to be widened and, although this
is a standard procedure in many births, the sense of violence is secured by cutting
to Carol Hathaway's anxious gaze at the procedure, followed by a close-up of
Jodi's face contorted in agony.

As Mark delivers the baby's head we see a close up of it, bloodied and small
against his hands that are (quite roughly) twisting it:

Mark: Damn!
Susan: Get him out!
Mark: He's stuck!

We cut to the growing horror on Jodi's face, as Mark explains that there is a
shoulder dystocia, 'the baby's shoulder is hung up on the pubic bone', reinforcing
the idea of Jodi herself as an obstruction. What is already an action sequence
then moves up a gear as further alarms go off, and Chen – now very distressed
– whispers 'Oh my God.' There follow several minutes of Mark fighting with
Jodi's body to remove the baby: he begins 'the McRoberts manoeuvre', asking
the staff to push Jodi's legs right up to her chest, a process that elicits screams
from Jodi. We hear sounds of slick tissue being moved and joints creaking as
Mark battles to wrest the baby out without success: 'It's jammed! Page OB!'
Faced with an obstinate vagina Mark decides to 'extend the episiotomy', and we
see the absolute terror on Chen's face as she looks on and Carter turning his
head away in revulsion; but the baby remains 'jammed in'. Mark decides to push
the baby back inside – another shot of its head being roughly treated – and move
Jodi to the trauma room for an emergency Caesarian section. We then get a brief
moment of reflection as Sean berates Mark for his apparent indecision and Mark
tries to defend himself, using his bloodied hands to underline his arguments:

Mark: Grab a Caesarean tray – run – take her to trauma one, find out if Benton's
    still here, throw a sheet over her.
Sean: Where are you taking her?

Mark: We've got to do an emergency c-section – I need your consent.
Sean: You don't know what the hell you're doing! Have you ever done this before?
Mark: I've scrubbed in many times …
Sean: I want somebody else in here!
Mark: Look, we can't wait; if we wait five more minutes your baby's brain-dead.

Sean and the others go down the corridor with Jodi, who is wearing an oxygen mask effectively losing her voice, and appears a passive, dying woman. As they enter the swing doors of the trauma room Mark shuts out Sean.

From here we witness a remarkable sequence that exemplifies the astonishing choreography of action and camera mobility. It is similar to the virtuosity that we saw in the opening sequence of the episode, but this time there is the addition of the accumulation of dramatic force, since we know this story in detail. A continuous steadicam manoeuvre circles the table twice, each time displaying aspects of the treatment and associated character reactions.

After Mark leaves Sean looking through the windows of the swing door, we get a close-up of Jodi looking at the staff, clearly terrified; then we cut to a mobile shot of the trauma room as it begins two circles of the room.

If we take Jodi's head as 12 o'clock the camera is already moving at 11 when the shot begins, gliding towards the table, and taking in the brown antiseptic fluid being squirted over her pregnant abdomen. It moves through to 6, to pick up Mark and Susan, who has her hand between Jodi's legs and asks, 'What about anaesthesia?' Mark responds, 'There's no time, I'll throw in a local' with the camera still moving to 4 o'clock to pick up Chen as she cries, 'She's seizing!' The camera tracks more or less laterally to 1 o'clock again as Jodi writhes on the table, so as it completes its first circle it picks up Mark having his gloves put on by Carol. Its subsequent revolution is much nearer to the table and timed to pick up Carter's entrance into the room, reaching an 8 o'clock position to bring a frontal shot of Mark, using his wrist to push up his glasses and having to climb under some tubes. We see Carter run to get his gown, just as the camera pulls back to show Chen knocking over a tray of surgical instruments with a loud clatter.

Still in the same shot, the camera pauses on Mark as his gown is tied:

Mark: OK, everybody just take a deep breath, alright? *[Camera swings right to take in the hushed still staff, we hear the 'breathing' of a machine; then back to Mark]* … Somebody go up to the OB and physically *drag* somebody down here.

The shot takes us from an action sequence to one of reflection – Mark briefly seems to regain his authority and calm here, asking for more medication and sending one of the nurses out through the swing doors, which leaves us where we began at Sean's face. Nevertheless his request to 'drag somebody' from OB is a clear admission that he is *not* competent to continue, and this has the effect of destabilising our alignment with him. The mobile continuous observation that is the signature style of *ER* is not akin to documentary observation, but fluid and responsive, not reacting to or discovering events but seemingly prepared for them: the camera is part of this world not outside of it.

The next sequence is rendered with very fast cutting between Mark, Susan and the other medical staff who look on in horror. We see Mark hunched over Jodi's lower abdomen asking for a scalpel, unsure of where to make the incision. The confident medical terminology that previously was an index of the professional code is evaporating before our eyes: 'Is this the right place?' asks Mark. 'Yeah, yeah, that looks right,' Susan responds. When Mark asks Carol for the 'Metz' she looks back baffled before he simplifies it to, 'The long scissors.' Cut to Carter at Jodi's feet looking intently but also glancing between Susan and Mark, a student faced with teachers at the limits of their capabilities. As Mark begins cutting Susan remembers that there is 'something' about the bladder to which Mark's stunned expression is an admission that he doesn't know if he's cutting through it or not.

We get no shots of the incision itself, indeed, apart from Mark's bloody gloves and the shots of the baby's head, the sequence is relatively gore-free. But body horror is conveyed by a mixture of sounds, reactions and dialogue, leaving us in little doubt of the extent of the invasive procedures (*Mark:* I'm in. I'm dividing the peritoneum.). And immediately there is the contrast between this professional language and the simplified instruction: Mark tells Carol, Chen and Susan to 'grab that side and pull – I need exposure, pull!' They prise open Jodi's abdomen accompanied by horrific squelching and tearing sounds, Chen blinking uncontrollably and Carter again turning away in disgust with an 'Oh, man!' When the opening is wide enough Mark has to cut through the uterus, as if Jodi's body was a series of puzzles or barriers that have to be breached.

> *Mark:* You cut across the lower segment of the uterus.
> *Susan: [looks at him astonished]* You're asking me?
> *Mark:* I'm asking God. Suction.
> *Susan:* I don't think you're all the way through.
> *Mark: [shaking]* I don't want to cut the baby.

'Asking God' means both that Susan – any doctor – is not God, and that Mark is in the unwelcome position of playing God, having to make decisions that have a life or death impact on mother and baby. It seems that the malevolent working of fate and chance have placed him in that position, rather than his own wilful

'I'm asking God': Mark Greene
(Anthony Edwards) in *ER*, 'Love's
Labor Lost'

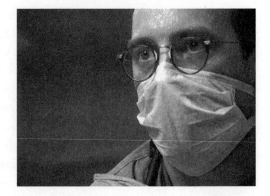

arrogance and confidence although, as we shall see, this is less clear cut than it seems.

There are more shots of Chen crying and Carter trying to look away as Mark starts to pull the baby out but the unruly woman's body has more surprises. Alarms go off and Mark once again invokes the cruel God:

> *Mark:* I'm in – Oh my God!
> *Susan:* She's bleeding out!

Jodi has severe internal bleeding and we get a high shot of Jodi's unconscious face, brightly lit, as the staff fight to infuse more blood and Mark tugs the baby out and reports that he is not breathing. Now that mother and child are in separate spaces treatment is divided in the trauma room. Mark saves the baby, and Carter is reduced to putting his hand in Jodi's abdomen to stop the aorta bleeding. After nearly twenty minutes of horror, things start to look up – Jodi is 'stable' (albeit with Carter's hand inside her) and the baby's condition is improving.

At this point the OB attending, Janet Coburn, bursts into the room appraising the scene with a mixture of bewilderment and disgust:

> *Coburn:* What's going on in here?
> *Mark:* I intubated, the baby went bad.
> *Coburn: [looking in astonishment at Carter]* Who is he and what's he doing in there?
> *Carter:* I'm John Carter, a med student, and I'm applying pressure to the aorta.
> *Coburn: [to Mark]* It's a damned mess – what did you use, a chainsaw? You should
> have let me know you were in over your head.

Coburn represents the reinstatement of professional authority but we may feel some sympathy with Mark since we have seen him trying to get help from OB. Coburn assists in stitching up Jodi, and Sean takes the baby, Jared, upstairs to

OB. There then follows an extended senior-junior reflection scene in the corridor outside:

> *Coburn:* I've never seen such a chain of errors of judgment.
> *Mark:* I did what you said.
> *Coburn:* You missed a pre-eclampsia, you underestimated the foetal weight.
> *Mark:* I was expecting OB backup.
> *Coburn:* You miss a placental abruption.
> *Mark:* What? *[Coburn hands him an ultrasound photo]*
> *Coburn:* Blood clot, right there. You do an ill-advised forceps delivery on a baby that's too big and then you do a hack job of a c-section.
> *Mark:* Look it was me in the barrel with the baby going down the tubes!
> *Coburn:* The only thing that saved you from disaster was dumb luck.
> *Mark:* Well if it wasn't for me the mother would be dead and the baby a vegetable.

Janet Coburn is a physical analogue of Mark's wife, Jenn, another career woman who articulates the feminist critique of medical care as a sublimated violence and removal of control over the woman's body. Here we are given competing explanations that trouble our alignment with Mark: for Mark is right to say that he did call (eventually) for backup, but the photographic fact that he missed Jodi's internal bleeding means that we have to acknowledge his own complicity in the trauma. This uncomfortable position is reinforced when Susan appears towards the end of the senior-junior exchange and reassures Mark that he has done the right thing:

> *Susan:* She's just covering herself.
> *Mark:* She was right, it's my screw up.
> *Susan:* You were great in there Mark. I couldn't have done that.
> *Mark:* It's my fault that she went sour, she's my patient.

'I've never seen such a chain of errors of judgment!': Janet Coburn (Amy Aquino) and Mark Greene (Anthony Edwards) argue in *ER*, 'Love's Labor Lost'

Susan: No one is going to blame you.
Mark: [very distressed] No, they don't have to.

The reflection scene is interrupted by a nurse shouting, 'She's crashing!' and the camera takes us to an already very bloody trauma room and a series of dissolves that relays Jodi's death in a medley of shots that emphasise Mark's strenuous efforts to revive her as he huffs and puffs over Jodi's immobile body. The final shot, reminiscent of Laura Palmer's aestheticised beauty when she is found dead in *Twin Peaks*, shows Jodi with a tube in her mouth and a small ribbon of blood around her nose. The alarms have been silenced and the only sounds are of Mark's heaving breathing as he desperately administers CPR to Jodi's chest, watched by the staff with looks of pity for him. Coburn calls time of death and Mark, with an expression of terror on his face, silently leaves the room and goes up to tell Sean the news of his wife's death.

Later we see Mark alone in the trauma room staring at Jodi's face; outside in the corridor a cleaning trolley is parked, a grim reminder that Jodi has become part of another hospital worker's routine duties. Carter walks inside and attempts to offer words of reassurance to Mark:

Carter: Dr Greene … I just wanted to say, er, or to tell you that, um, I thought what you did was a heroic thing.

As viewers we may well feel some of Carter's hesitancy since we are caught between competing interpretations with Carter's remark incongruent with our experience of the previous horror and with Mark's own understanding of it (he looks puzzled at the remark and leaves without a word). It suggests a sense of heroism that is a product of failure, the decision to go on when the world cruelly produces unfair and unsurpassable challenges. The episode ends with Mark refusing Susan's offer of ready reality in the form of a greasy breakfast – instead he chooses to go home alone on the train, weeping, as it passes bland buildings near the track.

While Jodi's case may represent the stubborn intransigence of the body that does not respond to treatment, it also acts as a surrogate reflector for the doctors/surgeons in that the failure of the body to recover reflects back on their own diminished potency, and in a wider sense it may represent their failure to overcome death and mortality. As I have hinted above, while we may feel considerable sympathy for Mark's plight, this is complicated by competing points of view that are insinuated into the drama. To a certain extent Mark's marital and professional problems are externalised onto the O'Briens. The break-up of his marriage because his wife wishes to pursue her own career is subtly paralleled

Beautiful death: Jodie O'Brien (Colleen
Flynn) in *ER*, 'Love's Labor Lost'

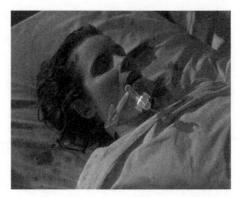

when Jodi, screaming in agony with labour pains, shouts at her husband, 'That
fantasy that I would stay at home and raise lots of kids – forget it, this is the only
one!' (Mark and his wife Jenn had only one child before they separated.) Indeed
the O'Briens' initially happy relationship changes as Jodi suffers more pain –
from the minor disagreement over names, to her telling Sean to 'Shut up!' as,
in the midst of her contractions, he tells her he loves her so much.

Mark's delegation of responsibility in asking other doctors and nurses to 'go
upstairs' to get help also seems odd since, as he admits during the second season
episode when the O'Brien case is the subject of litigation, he could have gone
up there himself, and his asking for OB backup becomes 'I'm asking God'. Thus,
the repeated references to drag someone from 'upstairs' seem to be another
subtle indication of his faith in higher forces as he loses control of his own
domain where before he walked confidently along the corridors dispensing
wisdom and telling jokes. His gradual loss of control is foreshadowed by the
events leading up to the O'Brien disaster, in particular the opening shots of the
gunshot victim being thrown from a car, indicating both concern to get a 'buddy'
for treatment and indifference to his injuries.

Similarly, the tattooed man that we see Carter and Mark speak with at the
beginning illustrates what is at stake in maintaining a relationship – Mr Longet
has used a power sander on his arm to remove a tattoo in order to please his new
partner, causing a severe abrasion on his right bicep, itself suggesting that
compromised masculinity is the price to pay for romance. Mark's solution – a
skin graft moving a serpent head onto the body of a goddess – implies that
Mark's relations with women extend to his demonisation of them, particularly if
we consider Mark's diminished potency in his relationships with powerful
women like Coburn, his wife Jenn and, to a certain extent, Jodi O'Brien.

'Love's Labor Lost' demonstrates that the intransigence of the body and the
failure of doctors to cope with it is the central concern of new hospital dramas,
rather than limits on medical resources. It also asks us to reframe our

understanding of failure and heroism as Mark's actions (or inactions) cannot be closed as either fully heroic or utterly destructive. Mark Greene is the natural successor to Alan Alda's Hawkeye in *M*A*S*H* as his character, although often lacking the spontaneous wit of the latter, seems doomed to follow an arc where the malign forces of fate and chance shape his view of the world. It is a world without God and without the possibility of playing that role; one that offers no solace, only hostile indifference. In the second season the episode 'It's Not Easy Being Greene'[7] begins with Mark jogging in a snow-swept Chicago, battling against the weather, and at the end of 'Love's Labor Lost' the view from the train offers no distractions, only bleak grey and white buildings.

Notes

1. *ER*, 'Love's Labor Lost', season 1, episode 18 (1994).
2. Other movie examples of this include *Extreme Measures* (Apted, 1996), *The Hospital* (Hiller, 1971), *Anatomie* (Ruzowitzky, 2000) and *Century* (Poliakoff, 1993). In *Century* a doctor systematically sterilises the indigent population of London.
3. *Cardiac Arrest*, 'The Body Electric', season 3, episode 1 (1996).
4. *ER*, 'Rampage', season 7, episode 22 (2000).
5. *ER*, 'Carter's Choice', season 4, episode 13 (1997).
6. Written by Lance A. Gentile and directed by Mimi Leder.
7. *ER*, 'It's Not Easy Being Greene', season 2, episode 13 (1995).

Conclusion

The new hospital dramas of the 1990s represented a significant development in the medical drama genre. Under the canopy of the growing medicalisation of everyday life they tapped into the body-centred fears and fascinations of an anxious age. Hospital drama drew on these discursive contexts to combine the realisation of the biological and melodramatic possibilities of the body in visual and narrative terms. Harnessing this to a serial form that followed the development of workplace relations over time and linking these to the graphic nature of medical treatment secured the success of the medical drama as a hybrid genre in the mid-1990s. They borrowed and modified visual styles from reality television and action and horror film genres in order to present a distinctive *mise en scène* of interior-based action (interior in the sense of inside the building and inside the body).

At the same time they explored the problems of a generation of doctors being trained and nurtured by another generation who were less confident than ever about their place in the world. The metaphor of the war zone extended beyond the treatment of injury to professional and interpersonal relationships with groups and factions pitted against one another – juniors and seniors, doctors and patients, medical staff and the administration, men and women. In the face of all this, doctors' confidence was never dramatised at a lower level, and the prospect of 'playing God' – far from a privileged opportunity – was seen with trepidation.

In Chapter 1 I argued that the new hospital dramas are part of the apocalyptic phase of the genre, one that foregrounds nihilism, self-destruction and despair. Why would this be a popular topic for television fiction? What is the fascination of watching bodies subjected to injury, horror and invasive treatment? Perhaps because it connects, not with voyeurism, but with a widespread feeling of immediate fear for the future and vulnerability in the immediate present. Hospital dramas may provide ambivalent pleasures for those in the West who fear for their bodies and what might happen to them, or who are equally fascinated by fantasies of their own destruction. Perhaps this is part of their connection to an authentic experience of the world? As Slavoj Žižek argues, the experience of authenticity in contemporary society now seems to demand extreme measures:

> Another emblematic figure ... is the so called 'cutter' – a widespread pathological phenomenon in the USA. There are two million of them, mostly women, but also men, who cut themselves with razors. Why? It has nothing to do with masochism or suicide. It's simply that they don't feel real as persons and the idea is: it's only through this pain and when you feel warm blood that you feel reconnected again.[1]

However, it seems that with the demise of *Gideon's Crossing* in 2000 the new hospital dramas have lost their place as the most dynamic genre on television. Arguably this has been taken up by reality television, the resurgence of crime fiction and telefantasy. However, I would suggest that the 'medicalisation of television' has, in fact, dispersed the medical gaze across most of its genres. Safety seems to be a central concern of many reality shows and in *The Sopranos* the mental health of the central 'everyman' gangster indicates that the medical discourse as an explanatory framework for character behaviour has been integrated into most dramas. Even telefantasies such as *Buffy the Vampire Slayer* place a strong emphasis on the potential vulnerabilities of the central characters and the wounds they often suffer.

It is also the case that shows such as *Buffy* and *The Sopranos* actually *continue* the developments made by hospital dramas of the 1990s, in particular their recognition and nurturing of an intelligent audience that could relish a continuing sophistication in exploring generic innovation and their multi-narrative, multi-character address. I have used textual examples to demonstrate how hospital dramas can present complex moral, romantic and ethical problems without resorting to crude methods of simple closure in their narratives. In Stanley Cavell's words, 'I am always saying that we must let the films themselves teach us how to look at them and how to think about them', and in the late twentieth and early twenty-first centuries this surely applies to television fiction as well.[2]

In fact the sophistication of television fiction from the mid-1990s on in addressing the growing interest in the body was as intense as that produced by academic scholarship on the body. Outside of scientific scholarship, scholarly interest in medicine has been produced within a vast range of disciplines – for example, medical anthropology, the sociology of health and various intersections of cultural studies and film studies (especially in relation to stars and action cinema) and there has been a feminist interest in the use of medical imaging technologies, some of it tied to developments in early cinema studies.[3] Many such studies draw on the work of Michel Foucault, seeing medical intervention as a means of disciplining and regulating the human body, 'to analyse, and reconfigure the transient, uncontrollable field of the body' theorised as part of the 'social management of bodies'.[4] Others draw on post-modern theory to consider the way in which the body is constructed by, or inscribed by, discourse, power and culture – literally the body as a blank page upon which various patterns of power are inscribed.

Hospital dramas frequently *enact* the Foucauldian readings – using patients' bodies as vehicles for dramatic material, and populating their emergency wards with regulated, traumatised, docile, worn and exhausted bodies. Emily Martin has argued that the medical profession often theorises the body in terms of warfare, but as we have seen, this has been recognised and explored by hospital dramas as a command metaphor since $M*A*S*H$.[5] There can be no doubt that in what Bryan Turner has called the emergence of a somatic society where the body dominates political debate, new hospital dramas constitute a powerful contribution to the cultural representation of the body in decline.[6]

Television fiction has the potential to amplify and refine the anxieties, hopes and despair of culture and society. We often discover through television dramas structures of feeling (and anxiety), ways of thinking and modes of behaviour that we recognise as congruent or adjacent with our own or with how we imagine other lives might be. At the same time television, like any art form, develops its own rules, conventions and ways of thinking in relation to its past. This is true for television fiction, particularly that set in the contemporary world, where the requirements of plausibility are often in tension with the necessity for dramatic invention, and the opportunities and constraints of genre and formula.

I want to conclude with two moments that illustrate new hospital drama's embrace and dramatisation of the apocalyptic sensibility that pervades the contemporary western psyche. The final episode of *Cardiac Arrest*, 'Death Do Us Part', is dominated by images of death and self-abuse:[7] Raj and James agree to give a lethal dose of diamorphine to a terminally ill patient who carries a DNR (do not revive) instruction; a mental patient posing as a locum doctor carries a 'smiley' badge attached to his syringe as he does his rounds in the wards, quietly murdering patients. Nobody notices his actions until the end, when he stabs and kills Andrew Collin. Moments before they realise they have a serial killer on their hands we see James and Raj outside the hospital (a rare exterior shot) sitting under a tree. It is night, and Raj's mother has just told him that his father (who has just suffered a heart attack) is unhappy with him: '"When will Rajesh settle down?" he asks, "When will he show some ambition?" And I have to say I don't know. You are such a disappointment to him. You disappoint everyone who cares for you.' Raj asks, 'James, do you think I'm a failure?' James replies, 'See that dog over there licking his nads without a care in the world? Do you think he's worried about his career prospects as a dog?' So the disgusting habits of the beast are envied for their simplicity and distance from the cares of the world, and the necessity of ambition as means of defining what we hope we might become. One of Raj's patients, seen earlier in the episode, was a young man who had chopped off his own finger, telling Raj that, 'I needed to have something missing before I could feel complete.' Raj repeats this doggerel to James as if it had some significance, but he doesn't seem sure.

Jed Mercurio aligns *Cardiac Arrest* with a particular self-hating 'grunge feeling' of the early to mid-1990s that was reflected in the casting of actors in their early twenties:

> That was really apparent when we came to casting it at first. They [the producers] were thinking of people in their thirties – [I said] no – they've got to be younger for realism. It was really about being a twenty-something bloke where everything you do is life threatening and all the women are nuts. I wanted it to be really grungy – Kurt Cobain's suicide was around that time – about people in their mid-twenties with no sense of belonging. That is what I thought the series was about.[8]

Kurt Cobain committed suicide in April 1994; the name of his group, Nirvana, is defined as a place or state of oblivion to care, pain or external reality, and their lyrics instil a sense of violent self-hatred, a desire to be left alone, and a rejection of orderliness and hierarchy. In *Cardiac Arrest* the absence of care for the junior doctors and for their patients becomes, in the final analysis, indifference towards the self and absence of self-care, with many of the characters facing death, failure or insanity. What saves the programme from unremitting bleakness is its use of comedy to assuage – but also punch home – the extraordinary futility of the contemporary world. When the elderly consultant Ernest Docherty is performing an endoscopy he is asked, 'What do you see, Mr D.?' 'The future.'

As I argued before, *ER*'s Mark Greene is in many ways the natural successor to *M*A*S*H*'s Hawkeye but he suffers more intensely and his community of work seems to offer no solace at his darkest moments. In an extraordinary display of generic inheritance, the fifth season of *ER* casts Alan Alda as Gabriel Lawrence, a senior ER doctor too reliant on his past experience and gradually losing his competence with the onset of Alzheimer's disease. Mark does not get along with him.

Mark gradually disintegrates and loses control as the seasons progress (until he finds what seems like security in marriage in season seven); at the end of season three he is the victim of a violent assault in the male restroom that might be read as the externalisation of his own rage and self-hatred (one might read

Scared of the violence inside: Mark Greene (Anthony Edwards) in *ER*, 'Ambush'

his brain tumour in the seventh season as a similar kind of self-attack). To some extent we could argue that *ER* enacts a process of mourning for the white male (and the white family) in decline, with Mark Greene as the central figure whose death in season eight from brain cancer provides a powerful metaphor for the sense of a world (and for a body) at war with its Self. In that respect Mark Greene in *ER* forshadowed later US dramas that include similar white male figures suffering from existential distress, in particular Tony Soprano in *The Sopranos* (HBO, 1999–) and Nate Fisher in *Six Feet Under* (HBO, 2001–).

At the end of the live episode of *ER*, 'Ambush', the documentary team who have been such an intrusive presence in the ER interviews Mark.[9] Without prompting, Mark presents his own case which is almost a perfect description of the change in the genre that new hospital dramas enacted, from reassurance to despair:

> *Mark:* Probably the best part of my job is that sometimes, working here, you can repair some of the violence, some of the bad things that happen to people. … And, yes, I was attacked right here in the hospital. The worst thing about it wasn't what it did to me. The worst thing is that it meant some of the world's violence leaked into our own ER. This is meant to be a safe place for fixing people. But, now; it's vulnerable. And as an ER doctor that's hard to accept.
> *Director [off-screen]:* It sounds frightening. Are you scared?
> *Mark:* Sure. Of losing control …
> *Director [off-screen]:* Control of what's outside?
> *Mark:* And what's in here.

Mark's comments show us that the violence in the world can be experienced externally and from the inside. At the time of writing the world seems gripped by anxieties, fears for personal safety, and pessimism about the future: all issues that were anticipated with excellence and clarity by the new hospital dramas.

Notes

1. 'One measure of true love is: you can insult the other', interview with Slavoj Žižek by Sabine Reul and Thomas Deichmann, *Spiked* 15 November 2001 <www.spiked-online.com>.

2. Stanley Cavell, *The Pursuits of Happiness* (Cambridge, MA: Harvard University Press, 1981).

3. I'm thinking of books such as Yvonne Tasker, *Spectacular Bodies* (London: Routledge, 1993), Paula A. Triechler, Lisa Cartwright and Constance Penley (eds), *The Visible Woman: Imaging Technologies, Gender, and Science* (New York, NY: New York University Press, 1998). A comprehensive bibliography on body-scholarship is, 'Beauty and the Body in Film, Television, and Popular Culture: A Bibliography', *The Velvet Light Trap*, no. 49 (Spring 2002).

4. Lisa Cartwright, *Screening the Body: Tracing Medicine's Visual Culture* (Minneapolis: University of Minnesota Press, 1995), p. xiii.

5. Emily Martin, 'Toward an anthropology of immunology: The body as nation-state', *Medical Anthropology Quarterly*, no. 4 (1990) pp. 410–26.

6. Quoted in Elizabeth Hallam, Jenny Hockey and Glennys Howarth, *Beyond the Body: Death and Social Identity* (London: Routledge, 1999).

7. *Cardiac Arrest*, 'Death Do Us Part', season 3, episode 13 (1996).

8. Jed Mercurio interview with Jason Jacobs (22 July 1997).

9. *ER*, 'Ambush', season 4, episode 1 (1997).

Bibliography

Allen, I., 'What Doctors Want from their Careers', in Isobel Allen, Philip Brown and Patricia Hughes (eds), *Choosing Tomorrow's Doctors* (London: Policy Studies Institute, 1997).

Allen, I., 'What Doctors Want', in Jamie Harrison and Tim van Zwanenberg (eds), *GP Tomorrow* (Abingdon: Radcliffe Medical Press, 1998).

Arroyo, J. (ed.), *Action/Spectacle Cinema* (London: BFI, 2000).

Bailey, S., '"Professional Television": Three (Super) Texts and a (Super) Genre', *The Velvet Light Trap*, no. 47 (Spring 2001).

Bailey, S., 'Beauty and the Body in Film, Television and Popular Culture: A Bibliography', *The Velvet Light Trap*, no. 49 (Spring 2002).

Beck, U., *Risk Society: Towards a New Modernity* (London: Sage, 1992).

Beck, U., *The Brave New World of Work* (Cambridge: Polity Press, 2000).

Briscoe, J., 'The skull beneath the skin', *The Guardian* (18 February 1997).

Brodkey, H., *The Wild Darkness: The Story of My Death* (London: Fourth Estate, 1996).

Brunsdon, C., 'Structure of anxiety: recent British television crime fiction', *Screen*, vol. 39, no. 3 (Autumn 1998).

Brunsdon, C., 'Post-feminism and shopping films', in *Screen Tastes* (London: Routledge, 1998).

Calcutt, A., *Arrested Development: Pop Culture and the Erosion of Adulthood* (London: Cassell, 1998).

Calcutt, A., *White Noise: An A–Z of the Contradictions of Cyberculture* (Houndmills: Macmillan, 1999).

Caldwell, J., *Televisuality: Style, Crisis and Authority in American Television* (New Brunswick, NJ: Rutgers University Press, 1995).

Caldwell, J., 'Steadicam', in Horace Newcomb (ed.), *The Encylopedia of Television*, vol. 3 (Chicago, IL: Fitzroy Dearborn, 1997).

Carter, M., 'Carry on, matron', *The Guardian* (15 September 2000) .

Cartwright, L., *Screening the Body: Tracing Medicine's Visual Culture* (Minneapolis: University of Minnesota Press, 1995).

Cartwright, L., 'Community and the public body in breast cancer media activism', *Cultural Studies*, vol. 12, no. 2 (1998) pp. 117–38.

Cassidy, J., and Taylor, D., 'Doctor, doctor, where can I get an aspirin', *The Guardian* (12 December 1997).

Cavell, S., *The Pursuits of Happiness* (Cambridge, MA: Harvard University Press, 1981).

Cavell, S., 'The Fact of Television', in *Themes Out of School: Effects and Causes* (Chicago, IL: University of Chicago Press, 1984).

Cleare, A., and Wessely, S., 'Just what the doctor ordered – more alcohol and sex', *British Medical Journal*, no. 315 (20 December 1997).

Creeber, G., *Dennis Potter: Between Two Worlds* (Houndmills: Macmillan, 1998).

Dovey, J., 'Reality TV', in Glen Creeber (ed.), *The Television Genre Book* (London: BFI, 2001).

Dyer, R., 'Entertainment and Utopia', *Movie*, no. 24 (Spring 1977).

Ellis, J., *Seeing Things: Television in the Age of Uncertainty* (London: I.B. Tauris, 2000).

Fitzpatrick, M., 'Healthy eating in a diseased society', *LM*, no. 75 (January 1995).

Fitzpatrick, M., *The Tyranny of Health: Doctors and the Regulation of Lifestyle* (London: Routledge, 2001).

Fukuyama, F., *The Great Disruption: Human Nature and the Reconstitution of Social Order* (New York, NY: Free Press, 1999).

Fukuyama, F., *Our Posthuman Future* (London: Profile Books, 2000).

Furedi, F., *Culture of Fear: Risk-Taking and the Morality of Low Expectation* (London: Cassell, 1997).

Furedi, F., 'Feeding off the culture of fear', *LM*, no. 119 (April 1999).

Giddens, A., *Modernity and Self Identity: Self and Society in the Late Modern Age* (Cambridge: Polity Press, 1991).

Giddens, A., *Runaway World: How Globalisation Is Reshaping Our Lives* (London: Profile Books, 1999).

Gordon, P. N., Williamson, S., and Lawler, P .G., 'As seen on TV: observational study of cardiopulmonary resuscitation in British television medical dramas', *British Medical Journal*, vol. 317 (19 September 1998).

Gripsrud, J., *The Dynasty Years* (London: Routledge, 1995).

Hallam, E., Hockey, J., and Howarth, G., *Beyond the Body: Death and Social Identity* (London: Routledge, 1999).

Halloran, J., *The Therapeutic State* (New York, NY: New York University Press, 1998).

Harrison, J., 'Post-modern Influences', in Jamie Harrison and Tim van Zwanenberg (eds), *GP Tomorrow* (Abingdon: Radcliffe Medical Press, 1998).

Harrison, J., and van Zwanenberg, T. (eds), *GP Tomorrow* (Abingdon: Radcliffe Medical Press, 1998).

Hawkins, J., *Cutting Edge: Art-Horror and the Horrific Avant-garde* (Minneapolis: University of Minnesota Press, 2000).

Holland, P., *The Television Handbook* (London: Routledge, 1997).

Hudson, R., 'Television in Britain: Description and Dissent', *Theatre Quarterly*, vol. 2, no. 6 (April–June 1972).

Jacobowitz, F., and Lippe, R., 'Todd Haynes' *Safe*: Illness as Metaphor in the 90s', *CineAction*, no. 43 (July 1997).

Jacobs, J., 'Gunfire', in Karl Frech (ed.) *Screen Violence* (London: Bloomsbury, 1996).

Jacobs, J., *The Intimate Screen: Early Television Drama* (Oxford: Oxford University Press, 2000).

Jacoby, R., *The End of Utopia: Politics and Culture in an Age of Apathy* (New York, NY: Basic Books, 1999).

Johnson, R., 'What seems to be the trouble?', *Radio Times* (16–22 April 1994).

Karpf, A., *Doctoring the Media* (London: Routledge, 1988).

Kingsley, H., *Casualty: The Inside Story* (London: BBC Books, 1993).

Kracauer, S., *From Caligari to Hitler* (Princeton, NJ; Princeton University Press, 1974).

Laurance, J., 'Doctor, doctor, you're not on my wavelength: medical schools must accept lower A-levels in order to avoid creating bored GPs', *The Independent* (20 August 1994).

Laurance, J., 'Video of surgery aims to shock rather than inform', *The Times* (28 August 1996).

Laurance, J., 'Young doctors alienated by clipboard culture NHS', *The Independent* (22 April 1997).

Lawson, M., 'Over here and doing fine', *New Statesman and Society* (24 May 1996).

Liebmann-Smith, J., and Rosen, S. L., 'The Presentation of Illness on Television', in Charles Winick, *Deviance and the Mass Media* (London: Sage Publications, 1978).

Lury, K., 'Television Performance: Being, Acting and "Corpsing"', *New Formations*, no. 26 (1995–6).

MacUre, J. (Jed Mercurio), 'Cold turkey for television's medics', *The Observer* (17 April 1994).

Marc, D., *Comic Visions: Television Comedy and American Culture*, second edition (Malden: Blackwell, 1997).

Martin, E., 'Toward an anthropology of immunology: The body as nation-state', *Medical Anthropology Quarterly*, no. 4 (1990).

Medhurst, A., 'Still hooked on pulse fiction', *The Sunday Times* (30 April 1995).

Moir, J., 'Oh, what a lovely ward!', *The Observer* (11 February 1996).

Naughton, J., 'Slick operation with sick jokes', *The Observer* (24 April 1994).

Nelson, R., *TV Drama in Transition: Forms, Values and Cultural Change* (Houndmills: Macmillan, 1997).

O'Reilly, J., 'The real macabre', *The Guardian* (3 July 1995).

Page Snyder, L., 'The Uninsured: Myths and Realities', *Issues in Science and Technology Online* (Winter 2001).

Perkins, V., 'Same Tune Again', *CineAction* (Winter 2001).

Perkins, V. F., *Film as Film* (Harmondsworth: Pelican, 1972).

Perkins, V. F., *The Magnificent Ambersons* (London: BFI, 1999).

Poole, S., 'Whoa! I gotta pumper!', *Times Literary Supplement* (2 February 1996).

Rampton, J., 'On the darker side of Dickens', *The Times* (10 April 1998).

Richard, P., McManus, C., and Allen, I., 'British doctors are not disappearing', *British Medical Journal*, no. 314 (31 May 1997).

San Martín, N., 'Must See TV: Programming Identity on NBC Thursdays', in Mark Jancovich and James Lyons (eds), *Quality Popular Television* (London: BFI, 2003).

Schatz, T., 'Workplace Programs', in Horace Newcomb (ed.), *The Encyclopedia of Television*, vol. 3 (Chicago, IL: Fitzroy Dearborn, 1997).

Shelley, J., 'Fatal attractions', *The Sunday Times* (13 September 1992).

Sherman, J., 'Surgeons were paid £1000 for videotapes of operations', *The Times* (27 August 1996).

Showalter, E., *Hystories: Hysterical Epidemics and Modern Media* (New York, NY: Columbia University Press, 1997).

Sontag, S., *Illness as Metaphor;* and, *AIDS and its Metaphors* (London: Penguin Books, 1991).

Tasker, Y., *Spectacular Bodies* (London: Routledge, 1993).

Thomas, D., *Beyond Genre: Melodrama, Comedy and Romance in Hollywood Films* (Moffat: Cameron Books, 2000).

Triechler, P. A., Cartwright, L., and Penley, C. (eds), *The Visible Woman: Imaging Technologies, Gender, and Science* (New York, NY: New York University Press, 1998).

Turner, B., *The Body and Society*, second edition (London: Sage, 1996).

Turow, J., *Playing Doctor: Television, Storytelling and Medical Power* (Oxford: Oxford University Press, 1989).

Watney, S., 'The political significance of statistics in the AIDS crisis: epidemiology, representation and re-gaying', in Joshua Oppenheimer and Helena Reckitt (eds), *Acting on AIDS, Sex, Drugs and Politics* (London: Serpent's Tail, 1997).

Williams, L., *Hard Core: Power, Pleasure and the 'Frenzy of the Visible'* (London: Pandora Press, 1990).

Williams, L., 'Film Bodies: Gender, Genre, and Excess', *Film Quarterly*, vol. 44, no. 4 (Summer 1991).

Williams, R., *Television: Technology and Cultural Form* (London: Fontana, 1974).

Wittgenstein, L., *Philosophical Investigations* (Oxford: Blackwell, 2000, first published 1953).

List of Illustrations

Whilst considerable effort has been made to correctly identify the copyright holders, this has not been possible in all cases. We apologise for any apparent negligence and any omissions or corrections brought to our attention will be remedied in any future editions.

Introduction: *ER*, Warner Brothers Television; *M*A*S*H*, 20th Century Fox; **Genre and Context:** *Dr Kildare*, Arena Productions/MGM Television; **The Body in Ruins:** *ER*; *Casualty*, BBC; **'See One, Do One, Teach One':** *ER*; *Cardiac Arrest*, Island World Productions; **Men, Women and Patients:** *Cardiac Arrest*; *ER*; **Playing God:** *ER*; **Conclusion:** *ER*.

Index

Characters are listed under actor names; *Italicised* page numbers denote illustrations; those in **bold** indicate detailed analysis; n = endnote (indexed only for background information, not citations)